Yes, Please.
Whatever!

Penny**Palmano**

The expert on modern manners

Yes, Please. Whatever!

How to get the best out of
your teenagers

HARPER
thorsons

HarperThorsons
An Imprint of HarperCollins*Publishers*
77–85 Fulham Palace Road
Hammersmith, London W6 8JB

The website address is: www.thorsonselement.com

and HarperThorsons are trademarks of
HarperCollins*Publishers* Limited

First published by HarperThorsons 2005

1 3 5 7 9 10 8 6 4 2

© Penny Palmano 2005
Illustrations: © Katherine Palmano 2005

Penny Palmano asserts the moral right to be
identified as the author of this work

A catalogue record for this book
is available from the British Library

ISBN 0 00 721044 2

Printed and bound in Great Britain by
Clays Limited, St Ives plc

In memory of my god-daughter
Clare

To
Katherine, Sam and Fran
You are all wonderful, please remain so
… now about your rooms

Contents

good manners and behaviour

teenage affairs

Acknowledgements

Many thanks to Katherine, my daughter, for drawing the cartoons (albeit at the ninth hour). Also to my step-daughter Fran, and to Sam, my son, for their comments. I would also like to thank Gregg Davies for his thoughtful Foreword. And finally, thanks to Carole Tonkinson at HarperThorsons for her encouragement and enthusiasm.

Foreword

'Manners maketh man.' This was the title of an essay I was given by Mr Lloyd-Jones in the final year of primary school. It would not be an uncommon question to ask why an 11-year-old boy was given such a tough academic task. It was certainly not because I was an intellectual marvel. The truth is much more prosaic. I had stuck two fingers up to the retreating back of the football teacher for picking Paul Parberry instead of the goal machine who was Melanie Ashley. Unfortunately, I was spotted by the terrifying giant Lloyd-Jones. Watching someone being punished by the Head of Balsa Wood Creativity was great sport as we marvelled at his ability to pick up a boy (never a perfect girl of course) with his left arm, tuck him under his left armpit so that both gluteal muscles were in the optimal position for the bear's paw that was stuck on to his right arm. I would have preferred this punishment: I had received it once and had found that as soon as you became desensitized to the tingling that moved in waves from your bottom to your toes it wasn't too bad. But this punishment … this was serious. How on earth was I going to do this in the 24 hours I had been given?

I admit that it was the fear of what Lloyd-Jones would do to me the next day that led me to admit my crime to my mum in a halting, pathetic voice that evening. Instead of the wind-tunnel of noise which I expected, my mum listened quietly to my story. She said that my demonstration in disagreeing with the selection had indeed been wholly inappropriate and that she would have to tell my dad when he arrived home. In the meantime I was not allowed out, given extra chores and told not to worry about the essay. The next morning, at breakfast, my dad handed me eight full sheets of writing. Each sheet was covered in beautifully crafted words, many of which I had never read in any Enid Blyton book. This is what I handed to Mr Lloyd-Jones. He asked me had I written this: I said no I hadn't. He accepted this statement without further comment. I found out much later in life that he had greatly admired the fact that, as a family, we had sorted out my problem.

It is an incident which is etched into my memory and has formed a basis for my approach in education and latterly in my parenting. It is an incident that brings together three important qualities: Trust, Honesty and Respect. These are traditional values which form a skeleton on which we can build a body of parenting skills. Ms Palmano's book helps us all, as parents, to focus on how we can assemble a positive relationship with our children based on good common-sense. It's also pretty useful for Headmasters!

Gregg Davies
Headmaster
Shiplake College
Henley-on-Thames

Enjoy (at least try to)

Just as I wanted to have well-behaved, polite children I could take out without running the risk of psychological help, I didn't want confrontations, slamming doors, arguments and having to constantly apologize for their behaviour as teenagers. I like a sense of calm in our home and I wanted them to be charming and good company, not the stereotypical teenagers that are constantly maligned and sidelined as some sort of curious species to be constantly criticized, poked fun at and a constant source of amusement and derision.

And so many parents seem quite resigned to the fact that their own teenager's opinions, sense of style, choice of friends, time-keeping and responsibilities is all part of a huge conspiratorial wind-up to test them to the limit.

Well, the good news is our children's teenage years need not be a time of endless arguments, belligerence and aggression.

Your child's transition from child to teenager should be welcomed and not dreaded as though you are about to make a pact with the devil and nurture a werewolf (although at times it may feel like that). Your children are reaching their final development stage, from that gorgeous little baby to who they are now with their own opinions and ideas. From the age of thirteen to eighteen you should delight in watching their ideas and thoughts mature. How your sixteen year old views the world, a totally different world to the one you knew at that age, is stimulating and even inspiring. Now's the time you hear of their hopes for their future, from the thirteen year old determined to be a pop diva to the same child five years later who wants to go into medicine; this is a fantastic time.

The child who has reached the start of puberty is not some sort of alien but your beautiful little baby, who you sat up with all night and happily let vomit all over you. (And yes, this may well happen again but it probably won't be milk!)

Their teenage behaviour is a barometer of how we dealt with them as children and how we deal with them now. So, always remember we only get the teenagers we deserve.

These final years will fly by (apart from on a few occasions) and soon your children will be gone – either to university, travelling, or out to work – and by then they have virtually left home. My daughter is now at university and sometimes I just go and throw wet towels on her bedroom floor to make it seem more like home.

So on the eve of your child's thirteenth birthday when you kiss them goodnight, remembering what a darling child they have been and wondering what tomorrow and the next seven years will hold, don't worry, relax, you can all enjoy it. Although admittedly some times will be more enjoyable than others!

one

Turning Point

Teenagers are half adult and half child and the needs of both must be met, regardless of the fact that they think they are fully adult and you are simply there to fill their every need, as chauffeur, bank, clothing and music sponsor.

Three factors which affect teenage behaviour are puberty, the struggle for independence and their under-developed prefrontal cortex (part of their brain). Any of these on their own could cause problems but the three together makes a potent cocktail which needs to be handled with care. Throw in to the boiling cauldron peer pressure, exams and new relationships and you may start to understand why they feel frustrated, angry, moody and unreasonable.

puberty

Puberty brings with it raging hormones, and anyone who has ever experienced bad PMT will know what hormones can do (even men experience it because they are usually on the receiving end!). Irritability, aggression, irrationality and even depression are all symptoms of fluctuating hormones. So try and empathize with their feelings, imagine

'Go out with my friend tonight? Why no, mother. I'd much
rather sit here and agree with you.'

PMT with serious attitude and suddenly you'll know how
they're feeling.

independence

When children become teenagers they enter another
development stage of battling for their independence. It's
the final push to wean themselves off you and at times this
can be very painful for parents. For the past twelve years
they wanted to be with you, now they want to be on their
own or with their friends. The key is to give teenagers
more control over their own lives and a wider freedom of

choice, while remaining supportive, reassuring, loving and still having boundaries in place.

the teenage brain

Now, in contrast to many parents' popular belief, teenagers **do** actually have brains, it's just that they don't function like an adult's and that's not out of our children's choice.

In the last ten years, neuroscientists have come up with some extremely interesting results which may go a long way towards explaining partly why our teenagers behave the way they do. For most of the past century, it has been assumed that the brain was fully mature by the time a child reached puberty and that teenage angst was caused by their need to assert their independence and fluctuating hormones.

Not unlike our adolescents' changing body shape, different regions of the brain mature at different times and the prefrontal cortex, which has been likened to the brain police, does not fully develop until early twenties. This region of the brain checks all the information coming from other parts of the brain before releasing it. For instance, we might read something which will arouse a murderous rage in us, but the prefrontal cortex will come along and tell that part of the brain to 'quieten down'.

As Karl Pibrab, the director of Brain Research and Informational Sciences at Radford University in Virginia, puts it, 'The prefrontal cortex is the seat of civilization.'

So until the prefrontal cortex is fully developed, most teenagers don't have the ability to make good judgements, control their emotions, prioritize, or multi-task, as in make the right decision between watching TV, ringing a friend, doing a chore they've been asked to do or finishing their homework. This means that they do not intentionally do the wrong thing just to wind parents up. As Richard Restak, a neuropsychiatrist and author of *The Secret Life of the Brain* said, 'The teenage brain is a work in progress that we're only beginning to understand.' (So what chance do *we* have?!)

Work by Marvin Zuckerman, a professor of psychology, has found that new experiences, especially those with an element of risk, tap into a part of the teenager's brain which links with emotional centres that produce feelings of intense pleasure. Add to that the research which shows that during adolescence, the temporary decline in the production of serotonin in their brain will probably make

'It's not my fault I haven't done my English, washed up or let the dog out – it's my under-developed prefrontal cortex!'

them act more impulsively, and you may begin to realize why our adolescents might still jump into a car with a friend who's had a drink despite our warnings.

Finally, findings of Francine Benes, a neuroscientist, show that one of the last developments of the adult brain is the nerve coating called myelin, which acts like the insulation on an electric cord, allowing electrical impulses to travel down a nerve quicker and more efficiently. That is why a toddler is less co-ordinated than a ten year old. But this process may not be complete until their early twenties. Some of these nerves that become sheathed during adolescence connect regions of the brain that control emotion, judgement and impulse control. This happens earlier in girls than boys, which probably explains why girls are more emotionally mature than boys, whose myelin levels may not reach the same level until the age of thirty. (Thirty? Surely scientists mean seventy!)

Healthy Sources of Stimulation

Trying new experiences is a normal and healthy part of growing up, and as parents we need to try and encourage fairly safe sources of stimulation. Where one child may find it in a drama production at school, another will prefer the excitement of a BMX trick bike, and some children will be lucky enough to go skiing, or diving. Unfortunately, many children don't have the option or encouragement to find a sport or interest to stimulate them, and resort to crime or drugs.

So try and encourage your teenagers to take up new interests if they don't already have any.

The good news is that if all this scientific research is proven over a length of time, even very troubled teenagers can still learn good judgement and restraint.

Anyway, even if all this scientific research is absolutely correct, it's best we don't let our teenagers know, otherwise every time we ask them why they haven't done their homework or cleared the dishes, they'll reply, 'But it's not my fault, mum, it's my under-developed prefrontal cortex!'

where does it all go wrong?

No teenagers are perfect, and to be honest if you had a fifteen-year-old daughter who sat at home every evening wearing the sensible clothes you had chosen, never rang or went out with her friends, agreed with your every opinion, never experimented with her hair and make-up, only listened to your music and kept her room perfect, would you be deliriously happy or seriously worried? Believe me, you should be seriously worried.

Adolescents are at the crossroads between being an adult and a child and it is highly frustrating for them (and you). It is a time when they realize they can be independent from their parents yet still need their guidance, love and support, not that they'll ever consciously accept that fact. All teenagers want to be adults but don't have the maturity to master adult behaviour. They will often act childishly yet take umbrage if treated like one. And teenagers positively luxuriate in a world of non-responsibility; they can sit in front of a TV all day without a care in the world, make themselves sandwiches and leave the bread, filling and plates all over the kitchen.

Adolescence is a time of experimentation, and difficulties arise when parents lose the balance between allowing their teenagers to experience their new independence whilst still setting boundaries.

Trusting your teenagers is the key to their self-respect and respect of you. Most conflicts between parents and teenagers will stem from small, simple matters, such as getting in late, school work, untidy bedrooms and not helping around the house; all issues which can be settled with negotiation and compromise. Teenagers only rebel when they have something to rebel against.

Parents simply cannot parent teenagers the same way they necessarily parented them as children; their behaviour must change if they want to change their teenager's behaviour.

For the past twelve years parents have guided and nurtured their children and now they have to step back in some areas. Although we are still there for love and support we must let our children learn new life skills, so we have to stop being over-protective or over-guiding in coping with every day problems. But teenagers still need boundaries as adolescence is a very confusing time and knowing their limits is comforting, although they may well occasionally cross them. Teenagers who are not given boundaries will be unhappy and feel depressed, although outwardly they would argue otherwise.

Many parents find it difficult to understand that, just because their adolescents choose to spend more time with their friends than they do with their family, they don't love them any less. They will love and respect us far more for accepting they are now independent of constant parental supervision and given more responsibility to prove it. Parents also find it difficult to adjust to the emotional distance some teenagers put between them, but again this is not because their love for their parents has changed, they are in their own way weaning themselves off us. Teenagers still seek their parents' approval and if parents are constantly criticizing them they will seek approval elsewhere. Adolescents will not turn to parents who constantly say, 'No,' routinely judge, order, criticize or are not open to negotiation.

Aggression – Yours!

There will be times when your frustration and anger boil over, your heart rate shoots up and you want to shout and scream and even shake or hit them. 'How could they have done that?' 'Why don't they ever do as they are asked?' 'Why don't they ever think of anyone but themselves?' 'Why do they have to leave such a bloody mess everywhere?' Overload can be sparked by the smallest issue, even a look or a shrug. First, it's normal to feel like this, you're a parent not Francis of Assisi. You have your own anxieties and stress from other parts of your life which will obviously overflow into how you deal with your teenagers on some days. When you get to overload, lock yourself in your bedroom, lie on the bed or go outside and take a five minute break. Take some deep breaths, look at a few photos of your teens when they were young children and smile, hard as this may seem. You might even have a good cry with the frustration of it all – well don't worry, you're not alone, we all feel like that sometimes. And don't feel guilty that you felt so mad you wanted to become physical; it was just anger. But it is much better to get yourself back under control before you tackle them over an issue. You can always resort to honesty, 'Come here and give me a hug to remind me why I love you, otherwise I may have to kill you.'

different priorities

Accept it, teenagers have different priorities to us. They are suddenly not very organized, or good time-keepers, their room is a mess, school is boring. Two things prioritize adolescents' minds: themselves and their friends.

'All you ever think about is yourself!' parents can be heard spitting at their teenagers. And to a point they're right, but they may as well shout, 'You're going through adolescence!' Teenagers do think about themselves, they do become more self-centred as they try and work out where they fit in, but messages are confusing, they live in a world that is constantly telling them to grow-up, but usually in a home where they are being treated like children. Society expects them to act in an adult way and yet nearly everything adult is illegal. They are very self-conscious of their changing shapes and voices, they feel insecure and the most important thing to them is fitting in with their friends. Above all, teenagers today need to feel they belong to a group. The group of friends they will be attracted to will be the group with the same interests in music, films, football, bands or whatever. And although they want to be individual they are very happy to conform to the code of dress or behaviour of their group of friends.

There are more pressures for this generation of teenagers than ever before: broken homes, drugs, academic achievement, alcohol and sex. And it is our generation that has inflicted this confused, pressurized attitude upon them.

With all this going on, they will naturally start to think more about themselves.

Today's teenagers are blamed for being too materialistic and a generation of consumers, but to a point whose fault is that? When we were growing up we got presents on birthdays and at Christmas, but this generation of children seem to have something new every few weeks, whether it's from parents who feel guilty at working long hours or who gave in too easily to their pleadings for a new DVD.

rule breakers

Teenagers love to experiment and cross boundaries. They want to show us that they are free of our control and in charge of their own lives. Suddenly, an adult world and everything that is associated with it, smoking, drinking, staying out late, porn movies, sex, drugs and rock 'n' roll are within arm's length (just remember these were even exciting to us once).

Very few children get through their teenage years without breaking the law in some way or another, like underage drinking, fake IDs, smoking, and some even get involved in more serious crimes such as stealing or drugs. But the good news is that statistically, teenage criminal behaviour seems to peak at around 17 and then disappear by adulthood.

'Wot?'

The bad news is, as parents you will have to live through this.

Adolescents break the law to appear grown up, to fit in with their peers, to impress their friends and, depending on your attitude, sometimes just to show you how independent and adult they are becoming, so the more you disapprove the more rebellious they may become.

They have to start making their own choices and decisions and finding out the consequences of certain actions. This is all part of finding out their identity and should be encouraged and supported, as trying to quash it will lead to huge ructions.

different types of parents

Have we all got such short memories that we have forgotten what we were like as teenagers? Or more to the point, are we horrified at the thought our own children will behave the way we did at that age? Now that is scary.

Depending on your age (and preference), your teenage years may have passed head-banging to Jimi Hendrix, The Doobie Brothers or the Bay City Rollers (okay, it's true, you can't head-bang to them). Whichever it was, I can pretty much guarantee that at some point a parent was shouting at you to 'turn that bloody music down', and we promised ourselves that when we had children we would never behave like that. We were all positive back then that we would always play music at decibels that left your head ringing. So what happened? We finally turned the music down, not because our parents told us to, but because it was too loud and we finally grew up. Your children will, too; the way they act and behave as adolescents is not how they will be as adults (hooray!).

So you're probably wondering why we all have to go through five years of stress. It is often reasoned that teenagers need to argue and battle with their parents on their journey to becoming an adult. Perhaps so, but is it really necessary to make everyone's life a total misery in the process? No.

It's all about the struggle for control – parents have it and children want it. It's the way we the parents deal with it that will make the difference to everyone's behaviour and sanity.

Parents' handling of their teens basically falls into one of five different categories. It's not rocket science to choose which one to aim for.

The Angry Parents

Their teens' behaviour drives parents to distraction and they resort to shouting, ordering, lecturing and saying such things as, what a disappointment they are, how bad or selfish they are, and asking what they did to deserve them.

'Stay calm!'

RESULT

Shouting at a teenager will produce one result: being shouted back at. Ordering will result in arguments, slamming doors, complete defiance and walking out. These parents are heading for a complete breakdown of communication with their adolescent. And constantly telling anyone – child, teen or adult – how bad they are will usually end up a self-fulfilling prophecy.

The Controlling Parents

These are parents who never let their teens take control of any part of their lives. They resist letting them take any responsibility or suffering any consequences for their actions.

RESULT

These teens grow up unable to make decisions or lead totally independent lives from their parents. If they are not allowed to learn that there are consequences for certain actions they will be incapable of accepting responsibility for their behaviour, creating complete nightmare adults.

The Abandoning Parents

When teens start to push away from their parents, these parents are more than happy to let them go, believing that their parenting days are over. These teenagers are left floundering with no support or guidance. They can see who they want, when they want and come and go with little to no supervision.

'Now, darling, when you're out tonight, I don't want you to
smoke or drink.'

RESULT

Hands-off parenting can have devastating results. It doubles the risk of teens smoking, taking drugs and drinking. The lack of loving, caring, supportive parents (or parent) can lead to violence, depression, anxieties and even mental health problems.

The Over-indulgent Parents

These parents did not put enough boundaries in place when their teenagers were children and gave them everything they wanted except positive attention and discipline. They run around after them and think their only needs are chauffeuring and money, which they satisfy generously.

RESULT

Teenagers are very disrespectful of their parents in the way they treat them and talk to them. These adolescents need proper communication with their parents instead of an open cheque book.

The Respectful Parents

These parents respect their teens by listening, setting boundaries, compromising, trusting, supporting and encouraging. These adolescents are given responsibility but are also taught that there are consequences to their actions.

RESULT

Teens who have a close bond with both or one parent and feel trusted, loved and supported, will usually have excellent relationships with their parents. (This fact has actually been proven by research into teenage behaviour.) These children will be able to experiment with their new independence and will develop and flourish within this supportive framework.

There are a few basics that every parent of a teenager should remember:

- Keep calm. If necessary, take several deep breaths before answering your teen's requests. Above all, avoid shouting.
- Don't be drawn into arguments, learn to bite your lip and walk away rather than have to get the last word in.
- Compromise and negotiate where possible to avoid using the word, 'No'; when you have to say it, mean it, and don't be bullied into changing your mind.
- Always try and use example to highlight issues rather than telling them outright.
- Avoid sarcasm.
- Keep a sense of humour, laughter is very de-stressing.
- Try and rephrase questions, such as, 'Have you done your homework yet?' to the less controlling, 'How's the homework coming on?'

When the going gets tough: sit down with a glass of wine
and remember how gorgeous they were at 5!

- Give them responsibility over their own behaviour whenever possible.
- Tell them you trust them to do the right thing.
- Try and be enthusiastic and positive about their friends, opinions and hopes.
- Avoid saying in any form, 'I told you so.' It's smug and unnecessary; after all, you should know better, you are the parent.
- Remember they still need your physical affection, just never show it in front of their friends.
- Try and empathize with what's going on in their head.
- Try and avoid constantly arguing with your partner in front of your children.
- Do not burden them with all your problems.
- Keep a supply of well-chilled wine in the fridge.

But above all, don't be scared to parent your teenager, they need you now more than ever.

what teenagers really need

What teenagers really need is love, respect, trust, support, understanding, encouragement and responsibility, and not the TV, computer, DVD, iPod, wardrobe full of designer clothes and unlimited allowance as they would lead you to believe.

The best way to help support your children through adolescence is to be involved in what's happening in their lives and talk to them on a daily basis. Even as teenagers your children need physical affection from you and they will still learn from example, so make sure you're always setting a good one.

Now that your teenagers are leading more independent lives you are less likely to be with them to demonstrate how they should behave. If you simply try and tell them a

These are what they **think** they need

list of dos and don'ts they will see you as being too controlling and probably ignore your advice.

The most successful way to convey your opinions and
expectations of their behaviour is by introducing different
subjects into conversations. The car or dinner table are
best for keeping their undivided attention.

Use examples of other teenagers' behaviour, or use
something you've read or experienced, or simply put
dilemmas to them to see what their reaction would be. For
instance, 'I was on the train the other day and there were
four teenagers sitting together, swearing loudly, eating
hamburgers and chips that stank the carriage out, and
then they left their rubbish on their seat when they left.
They were an absolute disgrace, everyone in the carriage
was disgusted with them.' 'How do you know we don't
behave like that on the train?' 'I know you know how to
behave and I don't believe that you would let yourselves or
me down like that. I have every faith in you to do the right
thing.'

By using examples to get your point across, your children learn how you feel about issues and how you would
expect them to react or behave in similar circumstances. It
also offers them the opportunity to ask hypothetical questions.

For example, 'You'll never believe this, I read in the
paper the other day that a sixteen year old had slept with
this boy and lied she was on the pill, as she hoped if she got
pregnant he would become her regular boyfriend. How
sad is that?' Daughters will usually be prompted to ask,
'What would you say if I said I was pregnant?' 'Well, first
darling, I would hope that you would wait until you are a

bit older than sixteen and definitely in a long-term relationship, then do the sensible thing, use contraception. But what a shame that poor girl was so naive to think that getting pregnant or having sex with someone is going to make him like her more. Boys will nearly always have sex with girls if it's on offer, but when they know a girl is that easy they seldom want her as a girlfriend.' 'But if the contraception didn't work and I was pregnant, would you throw me out?'

'There is nothing you could do that would make me throw you out, but I obviously wouldn't be delighted for your sake. It would restrict your future options so much, but if it happened we would work it out. You know you can always talk to me about anything, especially things that worry you.

Obviously the way you conduct your life and treat people will have just as big an impact on your teenager's behaviour as what you say.

And they need all the following probably more now than at any other time during their lives so far:

- Love and attention
- Respect
- Support
- Communication

two

Love and Attention

Showing unconditional love towards your children should never stop, whether they are two or thirty-two. It's just the way you and they demonstrate it that will change. They no longer want to sit on your lap with a bottle of warm milk and be told a story at six o'clock every evening; they would much rather sit on a friend's lap, guzzling crisps and fizzy drinks (or some sort of alcopop) watching some inherently violent film until three in the morning. But that's growing up for you.

Even as adults our needs change. Think back to when you were first married or living with your partner – you couldn't keep your hands off each other, any excuse, any where: the floor, the sofa, the shower, the kitchen table (pre-kids obviously). However, fourteen or fifteen years on you'd probably blush at the thought of the kitchen table: 'But I've just polished it!/What, with your back?/What, here and now, are you mad?' In fact, let's be honest, our idea of multiple orgasm would probably be a day on our own at a health spa being completely spoilt, cosseted and pampered with every treatment known to mankind while quaffing a glass or two of chilled champagne. But it doesn't mean we love our partners any less or our love has changed (well, hopefully not), it's just our needs.

And it's the same for the parents of teens; your love shouldn't change, it's just the way you demonstrate it that will. Your children still love you, they just may not show it in the way they used to. So, although the dynamics of your relationship have changed, that unconditional love must not, although you may feel it's being put to the test a few times.

Some parents with teens who are permanently at each other's throats can forget how much they love their children as they actually begin to think they dislike them. What they dislike, of course, is not them, it is their behaviour.

how to show love

Showing love to your teenager can be far more testing than showing love when they were little. Showering your cute three year old, who simply can't get enough of you anyway, with mushy kisses and cuddles was easy, but now what? Your teenager may dream of mushy kisses and cuddles, but sadly not from you any longer, but this is not to say they do not want physical affection from you, it's just the way that you demonstrate it will be different.

Children will obviously mature and hit puberty at different times, so there is no definite age when you can say any show of public affection must stop. But you'll soon realize the moment your child pulls away from the kiss on the cheek in public.

Physical Affection

First, a big no-no is trying to show any physical affection in front of their friends. So forget the goodbye kiss at school (in fact, if you're still doing the school run, they may even want to be dropped off a little distance away so they can saunter in on their own). In general, most teenagers don't want to be seen in public with their parents and especially not with any show of affection. A reassuring squeeze on their arm or a pat on the back will be enough.

Obviously, some children are less inhibited and in these cases will kiss you goodbye, which is great, but let your children lead in this area.

However, at home it is extremely important that physical contact is kept up. When they leave for and return from school, a hug and a kiss will be very welcome. Hugging is comforting and reassuring and reassurance is one thing teenagers need loads of. If you're watching TV in the evenings let them put their feet on you and give them a foot massage or put your arms around them or even just hold your daughter's hand.

It is so easy to overlook physical contact with growing children but it is vitally important to them.

When they are doing their homework or are in front of a computer screen, take a few minutes to give them a shoulder and neck massage. If they are upset about exam results, or not making the school team or having a rocky relationship, a good hug will help them to feel better. Also, whilst you are administering sympathetic hands, they are easier to talk to as they are less likely to move away.

Teenagers also become much more aware of their parents' relationship. And although seeing their parents kissing and even hugging will cause them enormous embarrassment, it is actually very healthy for them to see adult affection, that their parents are happy and at ease with each other.

Teenage sons often try and distance themselves from their mothers. Psychologists suggest it's not because their feelings have changed but because she is the only woman they have ever truly loved and now they are attracted to other women sexually, they distance themselves from their mother to avoid the possibility of having the slightest feelings towards her. This will change when they become more sexually focused. So although the mother may feel hurt, pleading, 'You don't love me anymore,' or, 'We used to be so close,' is fruitless. The teenage son has enough to contend with so a guilt trip from his mother is certainly not needed.

> **Fran:** 'Being out in a public place with your parents is sometimes embarrassing enough, attempts at hand holding and hugging is pushing it way too far and will most likely be rejected.'

Little Things Mean a Lot

We know that teenagers have different priorities to us and it seems that although most of our time is spent thinking and worrying about them, they seem to spend less than a

nanosecond thinking or worrying about us. They automatically assume and expect that as parents it is our job
to house, feed, educate, clothe them and chauffeur them
around. But it's the little things we do for them which will
get noticed, the small acts of kindness that in the larger
context will leave your teen feeling reassured and confident of your love.

Send text messages of 'Good luck' for exams, and 'Hope
you're feeling better' if they feel off colour or low. Cook
their favourite meal or buy their favourite treat after a success or a failure, however trivial it may seem. Help your
daughter tidy her room and then surprise her by putting a
vase of flowers in it. Make sure the outfit they plan to wear
at the weekend is clean and ready. If you realize they've
forgotten to take in their Science project, take it to school

Little things mean a lot

but, when you hand it over to them, rather than the lecture, 'Why are you so disorganized, you've got to learn ...' simply say with a smile, 'It's a good job I love you so much.'

These small acts of kindness will be remembered and are appreciated even if it is not mentioned at the time and eventually your child will start to emulate them by doing little thoughtful things for you and other people – not immediately, you understand, but eventually.

Do remember to actually tell them you love them, but not to tie it to a condition, 'I love you when you're home on time,' 'I love you when you work hard.' Always keep it unconditional, 'I love you.'

attention

Although teenagers will start to want their privacy and spend more time with their friends, they still need their parents' attention. Teenagers can still act up for attention if they are not receiving any and, just like young children, if they only ever receive attention when they misbehave, they will misbehave. So, if they start throwing their weight around or behaving in an immature, silly way, act just as you would with a toddler tantrum, and simply ignore it. Walk away, shut yourself in your room, never reward stupid behaviour with attention.

Give them attention by talking to them, discussing their interests and friends, or encouraging them to join you for a game, or ask to see them skateboard or show you their ball control, whatever it is they do well. And praise them when they are behaving well or simply just chilling out with their siblings without fighting or squabbling.

three

Respect

mutual respect

One of the biggest contributors to the problems parents have with their teenage children is the lack of respect they show (the parents, not the children!).

Parents constantly make demeaning comments within their earshot, such as, 'Oh, he's just going through a stage,' 'He's just being a Kevin,' 'Teenagers, they're all alike,' 'What does she know, she's just a child?' Any of these statements are likely to cause a severe breakdown in communication and so they should – how would you feel if someone said about you, 'Oh, she's just a housewife,' 'Typical, he's only a father,' 'What does she know, she's just a woman,' 'Pah, parents, they're all the same'? You'd no doubt be hopping mad and you certainly wouldn't respect the person who said it or anything else they said.

How can we possibly expect our growing children to show us any respect if we constantly disagree, nag, shout, moan, lecture and judge, not only to their faces but to others in their earshot?

Can you imagine if your boss complained about you to other members of staff and in front of everyone shouted at you how awful you were, adding that your attitude made him sick, he hated the way you dressed, but then what else should he expect from someone of your age? Would it make you want to:

a) Show enormous respect for your boss?
b) Try harder to please him?
c) Tell him to stick his job up his derrière?

Exactly, now had your boss taken you aside and talked his complaints through face to face, calmly, more diplomatically, and asked your opinion on how to improve things, don't you think it would have made a difference?

When your children were toddlers they had their own ideas and opinions, so obviously ten to twelve years down the line they have a few more which, regardless of whether you may or may not agree with them, you must respect. Whether it's clothes, music, friends or politics, they are entitled to form their own individual thoughts, even if you suspect they have been influenced by their friends, a particular celebrity, or a music video.

These years are the final push for teenagers towards becoming independent and leaving home to lead their own lives and it is a difficult time for many parents. Every aspect of their lives to date we have been heavily involved in, whether it was choosing the hand-embroidered smock dress or where they went to school, the parents' choice prevailed. But now your child no longer thinks your input is needed (apart from monetary and chauffeuring) it's hard to just sit back and let them make their own choices. But you simply must not try to quash or comment on every aspect of their lives.

The more we show our respect and trust in our teenagers the more they will reward us with their responsibility, and the more responsible they are the less stressed we are. They will soon realize that by showing us how responsible they are, they can have more freedom of choice.

The first time my son wanted to go to London on public transport I was concerned he was too young, but he said all his friends travelled on their own. So I relented, but asked that he ring me when he was just getting on the train, when he arrived in London and when he met up with his friends, and the same on his return. As he stuck to the agreement, it was fine and he was soon a regular commuter.

Explain to your teenagers that we want them to go and see their friends and have a good time, but our main concern is for their safety, and it is for that reason that we need to know where they are going and who they will be with.

And we do expect them to ask if they would like to go out or need a lift, with as much warning as possible.

Teenagers will rebel against lecturing, preaching, orders and being judged. Talk to them adult to adult. Even as adults they must realize that there are still rules and that there will be consequences if the rules are broken. For instance, if your teenager overspends on his mobile phone allowance, he will lose the use of it for a week. Although punishing teenagers can be tricky, if you start threatening an older teenager that they can't go out at the weekend they can walk out. If you cut down their allowance they might steal, and physical punishment is bullying, rarely has any affect and can lead to a physical struggle.

This is why it is important for teenagers to be given responsibility for their own actions. For example, if they leave their bike outside instead of putting it in the garage, and it gets stolen, it won't be replaced. As a parent you can be sympathetic, 'What a shame, there are so many dishonest people around, I'll get you up earlier for school as unfortunately you'll have to walk now, darling,' not the moaning, usual, 'I told you not to leave it out, I told you this would happen, now I'm going to have to get another one, do you think I'm made of money?'

> **Sam:** 'I do understand why parents get worried, but most times I wanted to do something that my parents were worried about, I would point out that I keep out of trouble and I am responsible. Sometimes I say, "Mum, you know you can trust me," because she can, and she lets me go.'

how to avoid arguments

Try and avoid head to head arguments. All they will achieve is bad feeling on both sides. Arguments often end up with shouting, unnecessary name-calling and accusations that both parties will later regret. Keep calm, don't swear, don't bring up past problems, respect and listen to what your child has to say. While your child is talking resist the temptation to interrupt, accuse or judge. Listen properly and respond. Always remember that you are the adult and they are the child, although I would strongly advise you never to point this out to them.

With any issue, sit down privately with your teen and work out between you a compromise that you are both happy with. For instance, if your teenager came home late without letting you know, instead of shouting, 'What sort of time do you think that was to come in? You are so irresponsible, you're not going out for a week,' try sitting down with them and explaining, 'I was so worried when you were late. You're a responsible person so please in future just ring me to let me know. And make sure your mobile is on so I can ring you.'

When you raise an issue with them, just stick to one thing at a time. If the immediate problem is poor results in recent school exams, discuss why and ways to solve it, don't drag in other issues … your room is always untidy … you don't help enough around the house. And avoid trying to get too personal, as that is not treating your children with the respect they deserve and you can hardly blame them for arguing back at you. Just as with small children, it is necessary to be clear that it is not the child who displeases but their behaviour or attitude you are not keen on.

Continually telling your teenager how awful they are is likely to become a self-fulfilling prophecy for them. However, if you tell them they are responsible and that you trust them, they are far less likely to let you down. Once they start going out with their friends, let them know what your expectations of them are, and what sort of an allowance they can have. Acknowledge that they may be drinking but to be sensible and not to come home and vomit in the hall. And if they do, they can clear it up.

Boys are not very good at arguing with any verbal dexterity and usually resort to name-calling or aggression to make their point, whereas girls are quite verbal and usually throw in a measure of emotion as well. Avoid being dragged into a drawn-out argument. The argument will usually be about something the teenager wants to do and the parent says, 'No.' First, the parent should listen calmly to the reasons put forward by the teenager as to why they should be able to do this certain thing, if necessary asking questions, and if the parent is absolutely positive their reply will still be 'No,' then the parent should tell them so, along with any reasons for coming to the decision. If you are in this situation, explain calmly, even apologize, that on this occasion the matter is no longer open for negotiation. Walk away. The matter is closed. Whatever the child replies, from cries of, 'You're so unfair,' to nastier name calling, you must not get dragged back in to the argument. Not unlike toddlers whose parents finally give in to their tantrums, teenagers will soon learn if they have the type of parents who will (after enough whining and moaning) change their mind. This will only lead to parents literally being bullied into changing their minds in the future. It is possible, of course, that circumstances may change (for instance, a friend's parent can give them a lift after all) which therefore eliminates the reason for the refusal. In this case, explain why you have had a change of mind.

A successful way to avoid the risk of an argument is to, whenever possible, hand the prerogative to the teenager, give them the responsibility for their own actions and immediate destiny. Get them to agree that they can go out with their friends but only after their history homework is finished. Then if the history homework fails to be done, they only have themselves to blame. If they start screaming and shouting, simply point out that they knew what the consequences were, the responsibility was theirs; this is what they agreed. End of story.

When one parent is engaged in 'discussions' with their teenager, it is imperative that the other parent doesn't get involved, especially if they are going to contradict what is already being said. Not only will this demean any parental authority and allow the teenager to see one parent as more reasonable, it will without doubt cause conflict between the parents, and the 'discussion' between parent and child can soon become a full-on argument between the two parents.

respecting their privacy

One of the first noticeable differences when your children become teenagers is their need for privacy and you will be showing your respect by allowing them this. Boys especially can spend hours on end in their room. However hard it is to accept they will suddenly want to spend time alone in their room, with their music, the very last thing they want is a parent barging into their room unannounced. Even siblings barging in will get shouted at, but your teenager will be far less impressed if you show up unannounced.

The respectful way is to knock on their door and announce who it is and ask if you can go in. WAIT for a reply – just because you have knocked does not mean you

Respect their privacy

can enter. They will usually reply, 'Yes,' or 'Just a minute.' If the reply is 'No,' and you need to speak, ask if they could come to the door and say what you need through the gap. Don't start whining, 'What are you doing in there that I can't see?' or 'Why can't I come in?' You asked the question, respect the answer. But if you can smell smoke or dope, ask them to come and see you (privately) in five minutes and then discuss it – don't bother to mention what it concerns as they will have time to invent replies.

Make sure all siblings know this house rule and obey it. And, of course, you should expect the same courtesy if any of your children want to come into your bedroom.

Sam: 'This can be a real issue and every teenager wants their privacy. I have many friends who get into huge arguments with their parents when they step in unannounced or knock and just barge in. It is totally disrespectful and kind of gives the impression that parents don't trust you. This is a really unnecessary cause of arguments.'

Diaries

Girls very often keep diaries to write down their feelings they may not wish to share with anyone else, including their parents, regardless of how close and open their relationship is as a family. Parents should never read their teenager's diary, however tempted they may feel. They may well read things that were written in a moment of stress or haste that will alarm them enough to prompt them to ask their child about its contents. As soon as they do the child will know that their parent has read their private diary. Regardless of the raised voices and arguments that will undoubtedly ensue, the trust between the parent and their child will have been broken. The result will be the teenager hiding their diary and being even more secretive than usual.

Fran: 'My real mum once read my diary, and then to make it worse, quoted comments from it in front of a big group of her friends. There was nothing that bad in it but the fact that she invaded my privacy like that really upset me.'

how to behave with friends

How Your Teenagers Should Behave with Your Friends

By the time your children are teenagers, good manners and behaviour should certainly be second nature.

If your teenagers are sitting watching TV or working at the computer and you enter with someone new for them to meet, they should stop what they are doing, stand up, shake hands and introduce themselves. As the parent you will probably add something about the visitor which your children should pick up on and ask a relevant question. If it is a family friend they should again stop what they are doing, stand up, either shake hands or kiss and make the effort to ask how they are or enquire if they've been on holiday and if so did they have a good time.

Sons and daughters should, without having to be asked, help lady guests and even men guests with their coats.

If a family friend visits and the parents are out, your teenagers should ask if they would like a soft drink or a cup of tea and talk to them until their parents return, not leave them on their own whilst they return to the TV.

Explain to your teens how important it is to show an interest in the person they are talking to and not just talk about themselves. It is also worth mentioning that at parties, however boring the person is they are talking to, they must keep eye contact and not let their eyes wander around looking for someone more interesting. To extricate themselves from the 'party bore' (which is usually the person who has nothing to say or only talks about themselves or their pet subject) rather than just walk off, they should politely say, with a smile, how enjoyable it was to talk to them and that they hope to see them later (not adding that this will preferably be from a distance).

How Teenagers Should Respect Their Friends

There is no time more important than adolescence for your teens to have friends. Teenage friends have tremendous influence over each other; they are like a halfway house between parents and being completely independent and replace parents in many areas. They discuss everything with their friends and look to their friends for approval, support and loyalty. Adolescents think alike, feel alike and they understand what each is going through. Friends don't stand in judgement as some parents do; they allow their friends just to be themselves. And teenagers need someone to share their innermost thoughts, feelings and anxieties with.

Thirteen and fourteen year olds crave popularity at school and acceptance by their circle of friends. Girls' relationships with their girlfriends are very emotional and that is the reason they can become so nasty and jealous. But this stage usually passes by the time they are fifteen and they settle into more relaxed, respectful relationships.

If your teenager seems worried about a friend of theirs, try and get them to discuss it with you and offer some helpful advice. If there is a suspicion that the friend has a problem with drugs or alcohol, suggest ways in which your teenager can help and remind them that ignoring the problem is never helping.

Teenagers tend to be very loyal to each other but if your child starts moaning to you about someone in particular, try and work out with your teen why that person is behaving in that way. After all, they are going to have a lifetime of meeting and working with people, so discussing why people behave the way they do is fairly interesting and sometimes quite intriguing.

How You Should Behave with Their Friends

Although teenagers may remark that other friend's parents are 'so cool' or 'legends', or that youngish mothers who wear even … 'younger' clothes look 'hot' or 'fit', what they actually want their own parents to be is 'normal'. 'Normal' is wearing normal clothes, not trying to look too fashionable or too young or even worse, too trendy. 'Normal' is ordinary language, not trying to talk in da lingo of teenagers and not trying to act or speak hip in front of their friends.

Treat their friends with respect, be polite and friendly, don't make embarrassing comments or criticize and don't reveal any information that your teenagers may have told you about them or ask any embarrassing questions. And don't disclose anything that you have been told about anyone else by your teenagers to your friends.

As for your own children, never say anything to their friends about an incident relating to them, their behaviour, anything they said about anyone else or anything that could be construed as embarrassing. Another 'no-no' is to put your children down in front of their friends, for instance, 'I wish you could talk some sense into Billy, I certainly can't get through to him.' Or 'I don't know why Billy can't have his hair the same length as yours instead of all over his face.' Comments like these will not only annoy and upset your own child but embarrass their friend.

You need to gain your teenager's trust that you can be amongst their friends and neither do nor say anything embarrassing. And don't be surprised when your teenagers don't want to be seen in public with you. It's not personal.

In my late teens a good friend of mine was distraught that her boyfriend had left her and the mere mention of his name would set her off in floods of tears. As she was coming to our home for supper I primed my parents not to say anything about it to her, but to talk of other things. They both guaranteed they wouldn't mention it. As soon as she arrived, the first thing my father said to her was, 'Hello Nicky, where did it all go wrong, then?'

Another time when I was sixteen, a guy I had fancied for months finally asked me to dance at a nightclub and drove me home. In our drive he had just leaned over for the kiss I had dreamt about for months when my father started flashing the outside light, then appeared in his pyjamas beckoning for me to go in. I was so embarrassed I could have died. I stormed past him and he seemed genuinely surprised that I was angry. Fathers!

Having Their Friends Around to Your Home

If you work at having a good relationship with your teenagers, they are more likely to bring their friends home. Actively encourage this so that you get to know your teenager's friends, and when your children are at your home with their friends, you know exactly where they are and with whom (two big worries out of the way!).

However, don't be surprised if when you first suggest they have some friends over they may be a bit hesitant because they don't want to be embarrassed (by you) and they still want to appear cool, so before they come around it's best to talk to your teenager about the visit to avoid any pitfalls. Don't forget, as this is your home and your domain, when your teenager has friends over, you will be the one doing most of the compromising.

First, explain to your teen what you would expect. Point out where their friends can put their coats and shoes (you may be a parent who doesn't want six pairs of size 10 trainers on your front doormat), that you would like to meet the friends, so before they disappear into a room they could pass by the kitchen to be introduced. Explain that you do not want to hear foul language emanating from their room which should be enough of a warning to make sure your teen keeps his or her friends under control.

WATCHING TV, CHILLING OUT

Whether they are going to watch TV or just chill out and listen to music, allocate a room for them, perhaps your teenager's bedroom if it's big enough or, if you're feeling generous, the sitting room. If it's going to be the bedroom, help your teenager pick up the clothes off the floor and give them some extra cushions or pillows to make it more comfortable for everyone.

Reassure them that you will not just barge in to the room, and that if you need to speak to them you will knock and wait, so under no circumstances will they lock their door. Discuss how loud they can have their music which will be acceptable to all. Explain to younger children that their older sibling will be having friends over and they can say hello, but they are to leave them in peace, and suggest that you can do something together.

FOOD AND DRINK

Tell your teen that you will supply some pizza/sandwiches/snacks and drinks.

Depending on their ages you may like to offer low-alcohol or normal beer. If they are going to have plates, glasses or mugs in the room, simply ask your teen if they would be kind enough to put them in the kitchen by the sink or in the dishwasher before they go. Make sure the waste bin is empty and tell your teen to make sure everyone puts their empty cans, crisp and snack wrappers in it. As it's your home, you may certainly insist on a smoking or alcohol ban in or out of your property.

When the friends arrive and come to say, 'Hello,' shake their hands and be welcoming, do not say anything to embarrass or demean your teenagers or their friends, as this is a sure-fire way of them never inviting anyone back again.

If, for any reason, you are unhappy once they are in the house, for instance the music is much louder than you agreed or you can hear swearing, knock on the door and ask for your teen to come out for a minute to see you, then explain the problem and ask them to rectify it. Once again, under no circumstances barge into the room and turn the music or TV off in front of them.

Make sure you say, 'Goodbye,' with a smile and not a scowl, and more than likely they will all thank you. Never say anything crass such as, 'I hope you all had a good time, Billy was so worried about having you all over, but now you can see we're not as bad as you thought, I hope you come again.' 'Goodbye, great to meet you all,' is enough.

How They Should Behave in Their Friends' Homes

Regardless of how your teenager's friends behave at your house, your concern is, how do your teenagers behave when they are in their friends' homes? Surprisingly, even quite young children, if they have been taught correctly at home, will behave extremely well in other people's homes. But as with most areas of their lives, teenagers should take on that little bit more responsibility. For instance, when they first arrive they should make the effort to go and see the parents, shake hands and ask how they are. If one parent is out but returns later and comes to say 'hello' when they are sitting down, they should stand up to shake hands.

If they have been invited for supper to their friend's house, remind them about their table manners and suggest that they help clear the table and offer to wash up. And if they stay the night ask the mother if she would like them to strip the bed. If she declines, they should leave the bed either made or turned down neatly.

It goes without saying that your teens must thank their hosts verbally or, depending on the situation, write a short letter of thanks.

parties for thirteen to fifteen year olds

In a way this is a harder age to please than sixteen pluses. Sixteen pluses want alcohol, music and the opposite sex. Many thirteen to fifteen year olds want exactly the same but for moral and legal reasons they can't have it, so an alternative needs to be found. They may also still be at the age where they want to invite the whole class, but personally that's not a good idea. Small is manageable. So unless your children come up with some workable ideas, offer some suggestions. For instance, you will treat six friends to the cinema, pizza supper and let them sleep over. Even at this age they may start asking if boys can sleep over, and your decision may well depend on your nervous system, the size of your house and compliance. If you agree, make it quite clear, boys in one room and girls in another. As a parent holding a mixed sleep-over you have a responsibility to the other parents to try and avoid the risk of exposing their children to sexual activity.

parties for sixteen years upwards

The inevitable time will come when you hear the words you knew you would always dread: 'Can I have some friends round for a party?' Your immediate thoughts will be of cigarette burns all over the furniture, gate-crashers, flour, beer and vomit all over the floor, broken basins and cisterns and the police being called to break up the public disturbance. So before you hit the 'Absolutely not, do you think I'm mad?' button, take three deep breaths and ask them to come and discuss it with you.

STEPS TO A SUCCESSFUL TEEN PARTY

1. First and foremost, they must agree to clear up after the party by a certain time the following day. If they don't agree willingly, negotiations are off.
2. Keep numbers low for the first party, about twelve to fifteen. If they say they want more, explain that if this party goes off without a hitch then the next time they can probably have more.
3. To avoid gate-crashers, ask them to invite their guests over the phone in the evening and to keep it to themselves, because if it gets around it will have to be cancelled.
4. Provide food to soak up any alcohol, like sandwiches, pizza, cheese and biscuits or bowls of Chinese/ Indian dishes and rice, or a big pasta dish and French bread.
5. Depending on their ages provide some limited alcohol and low alcohol beer, non-alcoholic wine and soft drinks and plenty of small individual bottles of water.

Take precautions to avoid gatecrashers

6. If you want to put some candles out make sure they are in storm lanterns so that they cannot easily be knocked over.
7. Work out how loud the music can be without annoying the neighbours.
8. Warn the neighbours.
9. If the neighbours are good friends suggest you all go out for supper.
10. Get younger siblings to stay with friends.
11. Sadly, it is a fact of life that many teenagers smoke, so either ban it completely or allocate a smoking area, if necessary outside (but away from being seen from the road) and provide ashtrays or allow them to smoke in one room (for example, the kitchen) only.

12. Tell them that if they see any of their friends getting the worse for wear, they should make sure they drink plenty of water as vomit is really nasty to clear up. Explain where the bucket, rubber gloves, paper towelling and cloths are, just in case.

13. Arrange a time that you will be home and a time by which you expect them to be gone.

14. If any are staying over, buy in some bacon and rolls so that your teen can make everyone breakfast before they start to clear up.

15. If they've had a good party and cleared up as agreed, congratulate and thank them for making it such a success.

Sam: 'However annoying cleaning up after a party is, it's well worth it because I was allowed to have more parties. I felt that my Mum was generous enough to allow me to have the party and get things ready so I wanted to keep to my part of the deal. My friends respect/worship my Mum for all the effort she always puts in and they don't mind helping to clean up in the morning.'

four

Support

food and diet

Our eating culture has changed since even a generation ago. In many homes, home-cooked meals around a table with the family have been replaced by eating fast-food, takeaways and processed meals often in solitude in front of the TV, and children are all the poorer for it.

During adolescence you will notice many changes in your teenagers' eating habits for which there are many reasons. The more understanding you have of the reasons, the easier it will be to support and benefit your growing children. Convincing your children to eat a healthy diet can feel like banging your head against a brick wall (repeatedly) but it is not, I have to add, impossible (or as painful!).

Always be a good example – it's no good sitting down to pizza and chips on a regular basis and telling your teenagers to eat a healthy diet. If you always provide a healthy meal, regardless of how simple, they will eat it. Obviously, there will be foods they prefer to others – that is normal – but, for instance, if they dislike a piece of fish they might enjoy fishcakes.

Provide a family meal, as often as possible, that everyone will enjoy, such as a roast, steak and home cooked oven chips, or tuna salad with a baked potato. If you can't think of simple healthy (quick) meals treat yourself to a cookbook that will provide them.

Suggest your children food shop with you one day to see if there is anything they see that they would like to try, as getting children interested in choosing food is the first step to getting them to eat healthily.

food and behaviour

Moodiness, lack of concentration, poor intellectual performance and disruptive behaviour can all be connected to a poor diet.

Recent reports have indicated that it is not only young children whose behaviour is affected by food. In 2002 *The British Journal of Psychiatry* published research of their findings in a controlled trial involving 230 young offenders. Half the offenders received supplements of vitamins, minerals and essential fatty acids and the other half received placebos. The group on the supplement committed 40 per cent fewer violent offences than the group taking the placebo and offending was down 25 per cent. Bernard Gesch, a senior research scientist in physiology at Oxford University, points out that nutrients are vital in the biochemical processes that produce serotonin and dopamine, brain transmitters which are known to affect mood.

High sugar-laden sweets, snacks and drinks can change the normal biochemical pathways, resulting in moody and disruptive behaviour. Products made from pure white flour will also convert into pure sugar with the same results.

High-fat or high-sugar meals can leave some people feeling very low after consumption. Schools that have taken out sweet vending machines and replaced them with fruit have found children more able to concentrate and less disruptive.

Growing Spurts

There will be times when you are simply amazed at the amount your children are eating. You may well wonder where can all that food possibly be going, but don't worry, continual grazing between meals is quite normal. Although half an hour after a proper meal they claim they are 'starving', they probably are. And unless they are grossly overweight, don't worry about it.

If you start to notice they are eating less it may be because their growing spurt is temporarily over and not necessarily because they are dieting (see Eating Disorders, page 198).

How to Help

Keep plenty of low-fat, low-sugar, healthy foods and snacks in the house. Healthy cereals (not the chocolate flavoured, high-salt, sugar-laden ones), brown bread, cheese, lean ham and cooked chicken, fresh fruit, nuts, yoghurt, ice-cream (check contents, it should have milk, eggs and cream – you'd be amazed at how many don't – plus flavourings), low-fat crisps and snacks, carrots, cherry tomatoes and cucumber sticks with low fat dips such as hummus. Try and stay clear of too many processed foods.

personal appearance

Unfortunately, everywhere we look, whether it is advertising hoardings, magazines or TV and films, unrealistic body shapes are looming down on us. Obviously our children are going to emulate their idols, boys wanting 'six-packs' and girls wanting to be a size 8 with breast implants. It is total madness, but sadly, here to stay for the foreseeable future. Our problem is how to encourage our children to eat for their present and future health and to help them feel satisfied with their own body.

How to Help

Raising their self-esteem is the first step towards a healthy goal. Parents using the words 'fat' or 'overweight' with regard to their children could possibly trigger a fast-track decision to dieting and possibly eating disorders.

Explain to your children that everyone's body shape develops at different times and maybe offer an example of someone they know and admire. Explain that even as adults your body shape can change, especially after having children – women with no bust before children can end up with a size D cup and visa versa. Try and make light of it and, if possible, tell them about the problems (you may have read about) their role models have had with their supposedly 'fantastic' figure. Girls do seem to worry more than boys, so it also doesn't hurt to explain that most guys don't like super slim girls, they prefer girls to have a shape.

Make sure that you compliment them on the way they look rather than criticize, and particularly praise one of their finest features, such as lovely thick hair, beautiful green eyes, good legs. If they moan about their fat waist, say things like, 'Well who's looking at your waist when you've got those fantastic legs?' Let's face it, none of us are perfect (far from it, in fact) but we all have some endearing feature to offset our bad bits, like short fat arms but good teeth, no neck but a great smile, fat hips but amazing long fingers. And your teenager needs to be praised and complimented on their great attributes.

Also praise and encourage other qualities apart from their physical appearance. Perhaps they are good artists, musicians, loyal friends, good listeners, great raconteurs. Building their self-esteem this way will help them to concentrate less on their appearance.

Insist the family sits around a table to eat if possible a minimum of three nights a week. Provide healthy meals.

a healthy diet

Breakfast: Exchange the sugar-laden, high-salt cereals for any of the following options. Low-salt, low-sugar or sugar-free cereals. Boiled, poached or scrambled egg and brown toast, fruit, porridge with skimmed milk or yoghurt and honey or brown sugar. Milkshakes or a 'smoothie' made from putting fruit and yoghurt in a blender, adding wheat-germ or bran if possible. Grilled bacon and tomatoes. Baked beans on brown toast. Brown toast and marmite, or banana or a good quality jam or marmalade.

Lunch: School lunches are a bête noir of mine. Why did the government continually harp on about children becoming obese but give the schools such an appallingly low budget per child that there is little option but to buy chips, burgers and pizzas? Finally, thanks to Jamie Oliver, it looks as though school lunches are about to improve.

Fortunately, some schools offer a healthy option, so suggest your children choose the healthy option and just have the chips or burgers once a week. Explain that hamburgers, pizza and chips are laden with fat and will make them sluggish during the afternoon.

Packed lunch: Brown bread or wholemeal pitta bread sandwiches, pasta salad, cheese, fruit, nuts, yoghurt and a bottle of water to drink.

Supper: Grilled or roasted meat, fish or chicken, egg dishes, baked potatoes, fresh vegetables, different salads, pastas, rice, pulses, cheese and yoghurt or fruit for dessert. Milk, water or juices with no added sugar.

skipping meals

How to Help

Never let children go without breakfast, it is one of the most important meals of the day. It should provide protein to kick start the brain and some good carbs to slowly release energy throughout the morning.

Teenagers will often say they are not hungry and skip a meal. If they eat regularly and you don't think they are doing it to try and lose weight, then it's okay, they may simply not be hungry. However, if you have just spent an hour preparing a meal for the whole family and at the last minute they decide they don't want to eat, then agree that if they are not hungry they don't have to eat, but you still expect them to sit at the table and join the rest of the family. Inevitably, once they are sitting with everyone else eating, if the serving dishes are on the table they may well help themselves to a little. Don't make any comments. Just enjoy.

If they say at the last minute that they will not be having supper with you and they can't sit with you because they are going out, point out that it is inconsiderate to not have let you know earlier. Explain that you will let them go this time, but in future you would expect an hour's notice (plus asking permission to go out) or they will only be allowed out (if at all) after they have sat with the rest of the family during supper, even if they choose not to eat.

If you suspect they are skipping meals to try and lose weight, explain that they will lose weight quicker by eating a low-fat meal, which you can provide, and by not eating they are simply tricking their body into believing there is no food and the body will automatically hold onto the fat, not knowing when it will next receive food.

change in diet

As children mature, so do their taste buds, and slowly or suddenly they will be up for trying new textures and flavours. They may have read about a certain food or tried it with their friends or seen a favourite TV or film celebrity eat it and wish to try it.

Teenagers, in their quest for independence and individuality, may also sometimes change their diet completely, just to prove to you that they are in control of what they do.

How to Help

When and if your children suggest they would like to try something new, for instance lamb couscous, rather than immediately dismiss the idea with a put down, 'Lamb couscous? This from the girl who thought a "capriccioso" pizza was a gourmet delicacy? Well, I can tell you now, you won't like it,' encourage them to try new dishes.

Many adolescents, for instance, will suddenly proclaim they have turned vegetarian. Rather than mocking their decision, pointing out that they must have eaten several cows in hamburgers in just the last two weeks alone or saying, 'If you think I'm cooking different meals every night, you are mistaken,' respect their decision and talk about what they will eat and are prepared to try on their new diet. Explain that to make their meals more interesting and varied they may like to try cooking a few things themselves while you're cooking the family meal. Show your willingness to go along with their new diet by suggesting that the whole family can have a couple of meat-free meals, which is a healthy option anyway. Treat them to a vegetarian cookbook.

As your teenagers get older they may start to eat more 'sophisticated' food with their friends' parents and surprise you by asking to get the same. Avocado pears, smoked salmon, mussels, pasta with chilli, whatever it is, say how delighted you are that they have found something new that they enjoy and agree to get some for the whole family.

Once they have started eating new flavours and trying new dishes, remark how pleased you are and suggest taking them out perhaps to your favourite restaurant, leaving younger siblings at home. They are growing up, so treat them as such.

Comfort Eating

We've all been there, feeling low and depressed. And the first thing we do is hit the biscuit tin then feel more depressed that we ate most of the contents. As we would much prefer that our children never turn to food for comfort, try to avoid giving them treats as a consolation when they are upset or depressed. Try and start a new regime of going for a walk or some other type of exercise if they are feeling low. The fresh air and exercise will immediately start to make you feel better.

exercise

Changes to Body Shape

Thanks to permanent media exposure of supposedly idealized body shapes of women and men, nearly all teenage girls and some boys are concerned about their weight. Explain to them that it is perfectly normal to gain some weight and experience normal physical changes during puberty. Suggest a healthy diet and exercise programme for them to follow and help them achieve it by having healthy snacks and plenty of fruit in the home.

Compliment your children on their shape and never, ever comment that they are overweight or fat, as that is a sure way to start eating problems. If you feel your children are overweight, make sure they have a healthy calorie-controlled supper and don't keep any high-fat, high-sugar snacks in the house, and they will appreciate your support and understanding. Energetic walking is one of the best exercises they can do, so perhaps they could start walking to school or part way to school. Or suggest they join a local fitness centre or take up jogging.

If your teen has always been in a sports team at school you may find that during puberty they decide to drop out, so point out that although you can do nothing to change their decision, they will be letting their side down as they were a valuable member of that team.

Take up New Activities

Encourage your teenagers to take up a new sport or activity. Martial arts are good for exercise and self-defence for either sex. Kick boxing is again good for both. Suggest to your daughter that you both join a gym or Pilates class if you are both interested in keeping fit. Look in your local paper and see what is on offer, but remember, you can only suggest to your teenagers that they take up an activity, and the more you press it the less likely they will.

teenage health issues

Periods

When your daughters start their periods they are just as likely to suffer from PMT (pre-menstrual tension) as we are, so be aware and be sympathetic. Your daughter may not even realize she is suffering from PMT so explain to her if you think she is and why it's happening and that she's not alone.

If she suffers from period pains, make sure there are always pain relievers in the home and offer hot water bottles and back rubs to help.

Acne

In a society that teaches us the importance of physical appearance, an outbreak of acne can seriously affect the confidence of your teenage children. They can become withdrawn and even depressed about it. First, to help them to understand, explain that 85 per cent of teenagers suffer from acne which is caused during the onset of puberty when the body begins to produce hormones called androgens. Boys tend to produce more of these hormones which is why their acne is usually more severe.

The myth that diet, especially chocolate and greasy foods, causes acne, is unfounded, although research has shown that bread may trigger it. American scientists believe the refined grain and sugar in some bread can cause high levels of insulin and past research has indicated that too much insulin can cause acne. Stimulants have also been shown to aggravate acne so suggest to your teenagers that they cut out alcohol, caffeine, nuts and shellfish.

On the outset of acne, take your teenager to the doctor to seek treatment.

How to help

Don't dismiss your children's worries about the onslaught of acne with, 'Oh don't worry, everyone gets it.' They don't care about everyone; they care about how awful they look with it.

It is important that you keep up your acne sufferer's self-esteem by telling them that people aren't worried about a few spots, it's who they are that's important, and their friends are not going to desert them because of some hormonal side-effect. Offer to buy them a tinted dermatological cream to help camouflage the spots, even for the boys, then if someone at school says, 'Hey, you're wearing make-up,' they can truthfully say that it's a medicated cream. Even offer to treat them to a haircut/blow dry at the hairdressers so that they have something positive they can focus on.

What They Can Do to Help

They should wash their face twice a day with a mild soap, avoiding high concentrates of alcohol products. Soaps containing benzoyl peroxide and salicylic acid are helpful for greasy skin but are too harsh for dry skin. They should also avoid too much rubbing or harsh exfoliating.

They should also wash their hair daily. Touching greasy hair and then their faces will only make the acne worse. And tell them to try to avoid squeezing and picking the spots as this will only inflame them, spread infection and increase the chance of scarring.

mood swings and teenage depression

Normal teenage mood swings can range from being over-cheerful and confident to thoroughly fed up, despondent and non-communicative all in one day. These swings can manifest themselves in frustration and anger resulting in shouting and slamming doors. The family is usually the main target, because after all this is all obviously your fault.

As with many facets of teenage life, stay calm and take a few deep breaths before reacting. Underreact rather than overreact as, in a way, these teenagers simply can't help themselves, their raging hormones are causing them to feel frustrated, irritable, angry and they know whatever they say, shout or scream at you, you will still love them. So first, don't shout back or be drawn into an argument. Let them shut themselves in their bedroom and perhaps take them up a drink after about ten minutes. Explain that you know they feel rough but screaming and shouting at family

The Mood-swingometer

members is really not on, it just causes upset with younger siblings. Tell them that as you always show them respect by not shouting, you expect the same respect and don't appreciate being shouted at. Then ask if there is anything in particular upsetting or worrying them to cause this outburst, tell them that if they want to talk you are there for them and explain that talking about a problem suddenly makes it appear less serious.

Mood swings will make life difficult for you and your suffering teenager, but they will eventually pass. However, persistent depression which begins to interfere with their normal lives may be caused by more serious adolescent depression and require professional advice.

The causes of teenage depression can range from anything from poor family relationships to stress.

Warning Signs to Look Out for

FEELINGS OF DESPAIR AND HOPELESSNESS

Teens can often feel negative about themselves and their future; that there's no point in anything. They may cry for no apparent reason. If your children ever talk about killing themselves, or wanting to hurt themselves, take it seriously. Never reply to statements like that with dismissive comments.

POOR PERFORMANCE AND LACK OF CONCENTRATION

This can be seen in a sudden drop in school grades and an inability to concentrate; withdrawing from school activities; playing truant or suddenly causing trouble at school, and withdrawing from friends and family.

Your teens may start spending time alone instead of with their friends and dropping interests.

LOW SELF-ESTEEM

Feelings of failure and not being able to live up to parental expectations are all signs of low self-esteem. So are sudden changes in eating and/or sleeping patterns.

Sleeping during the day, unable to get up for school (more than the normal) and disturbed sleep are all signs of depression. Sudden change in diet may be the trigger signs of an eating disorder.

How to Help

If you notice any of these changes are prolonged, take your teen aside to a quiet space where you will not be disturbed. Show that you care by taking them seriously. Sit down, hold their hand or put an arm around them and talk to them, ask very open ended questions and listen.

Never presume that you know the reason for your child's depression, it could be a singular factor that triggered it or a combination of reasons. Depression is caused by chemical imbalances in the brain and is far more common in children and teenagers than they may think.

Build up their self-esteem by pointing out their good points and why they have so many good friends and how you are all there to help and support.

If you have just divorced or a member of the family has died, speak to your teenager about it. Explain, especially with divorce, how sad for everyone it is that the marriage has broken down but they are loved by both parents regardless, and never talk badly about your ex in front of your children, or if they can overhear.

Explain that you are always there for them if they want to talk, that there is nothing, however shameful or terrible, they can't tell you. And you are there if they just want to sit and have a hug.

Try not to pressurize your teens into expecting they have to achieve fantastic grades or make the firsts in the sports teams. Let them know that as long as they do their best, that's good enough for you, and that you will always love them unconditionally, it will never be linked to performance.

Don't be afraid or embarrassed to contact professional help if you think your child needs it.

self-esteem and encouragement

Personal

The very word self-esteem is enough to make many parents want to scream.

Parenting books went through a phase of advising parents to shower their children with praise and reward from morning till night to increase their self-esteem, creating a generation of 'adulation addicts' who mistakenly thought they could do no wrong and could take only praise not criticism. These children were complete pains in the butt who showed little respect for anyone or anything, with little grasp of reality. Sadly, through no fault of their own, they grew into disrespectful, rude teenagers, but despite their worshipping parents will still suffer from the same

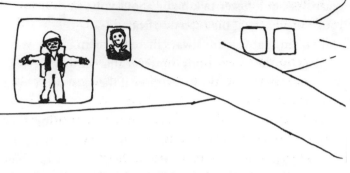

'I used to really enjoy skydiving, before I broke my legs ...
Anyway, I'm sure you'll love it ... Now jump!'

anxieties as other adolescents. However, it is important to build adolescents' self-esteem and self-respect by giving praise and constructive criticism when necessary.

Once they become teenagers, however confident your teenager may appear outwardly, the majority of adolescents are suffering from lack of confidence and anxiety about a host of issues from changing body shapes to where they fit into the world. So never be fooled into thinking because you have a cocky arrogant teenager they don't suffer from lack of confidence.

Adolescence is fraught with issues to lower self-esteem, from a break-out of spots, to being rejected by a boy or girlfriend, failing an exam, being dropped from the sports team and developing breasts. Only by forming or maintaining a close relationship with your teenagers will you be able to tell when there is a dip in confidence. Teenagers, not unlike toddlers, can behave in an exhibitionist way to overcome nervousness, or suddenly do something we would regard as childish or stupid to cover up their real anxieties.

The way to build up your child's self-esteem is to support them and remember to compliment rather than criticize.

Up to now, we have been involved in their choices but once teens start choosing their own clothes, hairstyle, music, friends and lifestyle (to a degree) it is very easy to constantly criticize without offering the slightest praise.

'You're not going out looking like that are you?'

'Can't you do something with your hair?'

'Those jeans are awful.'

'Oh my god, what do you look like?'

'I just don't like those new friends of yours.'

Sound familiar? Here they are desperately trying to be individual, coping with hormones, peer pressure and trying to fit in and here we are being completely negative. Before we open our mouths to criticize, we should try and empathize how we would feel if someone said it to us. Imagine we've just spent an hour getting ready for a very important evening (every social date is important to teenagers), tried on five different outfits, slapped on the make-up, fussed over the hair and just when we think we're looking great, before we set foot outside the door, our partner says in a disgusted voice, 'You're not going to wear that are you, it makes you look fat!' Would that really make us feel confident or turn us into a nervous wreck or, worse, a very aggressive nervous wreck? However, if someone said, 'That looks fine but you looked sensational in that red dress you wore the other week,' you'd think, 'Okay, so I'll change and wear the red dress and leave the house feeling confident that I look sensational.'

> When I was about sixteen I complained to my mother about the lines appearing on my forehead. My mother said not to worry, she would give me some moisturizer to apply and it was probably because I had dry skin. My father, overhearing, said I was not to worry as I could, 'Screw my school hat on so it wouldn't blow off in a strong wind'. He thought this hilariously funny, but sadly I didn't.

Academic

Whether it's GCSEs, AS and A2 levels (A levels to us) or Key stages, the British education system just can't seem to get enough of examining our youth, and just at a time when academic studies come so low in their list of priorities. New relationships, music, hair and clothes are just *soooo* much more important and fun than physics (even we know that's true), but now is the time our children have to start buckling down to pass all these wretched exams.

And when we see our adolescents watching TV or listening to their music rather than tackling their maths homework, we do become concerned and it is very easy, even human nature, to make comments such as:

'You'd better start working hard if you want to do half as well as your brother.'

'Your friend Annie has made the school orchestra. She must be really good – I don't know why you haven't, you've been playing the piano for years, you just never practise enough!'

'Billy's mum told me he's in the football team. I don't know why you never make it to the team.'

'Your brother wants to be a doctor, we know you're not as clever as him but what do you think you are going to do?'

'Your sister's got one A*, five A's and three B's, I can't see you getting such good grades.'

We say things like this to try and motivate our youngsters into action, but comments like these can easily do the opposite and de-motivate them. No child or adult wants to be constantly compared to someone much brighter and cleverer or more capable; it would be like your partner saying things such as:

'Your sister's a fantastic cook, you must get her recipe for that pasta dish we had and then perhaps you could try it?'

'Katy is amazing, the way she works, has great kids and throws fantastic supper parties. Wouldn't you like to be that organized?'

Constant comments like these would undermine our confidence (plus really anger us), just as the following comments could undermine our partners confidence:

'Why did Bob get the promotion and not you, he must be so good at his job.'

'Jack next door told me he'd stripped down his carburettor and I said you couldn't even change a tyre.'

Teenagers are no different from adults in enjoying praise and encouragement and as they develop and learn new skills, words of encouragement spur them on to try even harder. They also need the confidence to tackle new situations and challenges. Not everyone is academic;

school exam results should not be the benchmark by which children are judged as failures or successes.

If your child struggles with academic work, sympathize with them and point out their good points, such as:

'Well, darling, I know you find maths difficult, but better to have your personality than a great brain for maths. You won't find many girls entertained talking about logarithms.'

'So what if you don't have a scientific brain, you are so artistic, and that is something that you can always use, whether it's your career, decorating your first flat, or the way you wrap up presents, and friends will always notice.'

And in reply to their protestations about not being as clever as their siblings: 'So what if your brother wants to be a doctor, that's what he wants to do. Whatever you choose to do is equally important and you will do equally well, and on the plus side you won't have to put your finger up anyone's bottom.'

Low self-esteem is the root to so many teenage problems, try and ensure in a responsible, realistic way, that it doesn't happen to yours.

Sam: 'Never demotivate or put down a child. I have a particular friend who is always put down by his parents and some of his friends. His parents also compare him to his 'perfect' brother. I find he now never has any self-belief or confidence, which is a real shame.'

Monetary

'Do you think I'm made of money?' 'You mean you've run out again, already?' Sound familiar? No doubt your parents at some point said these things to you and now you are saying them, perhaps fairly regularly, to your teenagers. Let's not forget that as parents it is our responsibility to teach our children to be independent so they can venture out into the world equipped with life skills, so giving them money every time they run out is extremely irresponsible of us.

We have to allow them to learn how to budget and live within their means and the only way teenagers will ever learn this is by being given an allowance.

If only!

Some children are naturally good with money while others are completely hopeless and these days, when most children get presents and gifts outside of celebrations, they derive little education about the value of money or the concept of saving.

allowance

Although your children have probably had a small amount of weekly pocket money, as soon as they reach thirteen or fourteen, you need to start giving them an allowance on a weekly basis for several reasons:

- They will start to realize the value of money and buy what they want from their limited budget or even ... save ... for something (be warned, neither of these two things will happen overnight).
- You will know exactly how much you are giving them weekly and will have an idea of what they can afford with that money.
- It will prevent you being angry every time they ask for money and using tired old clichés that you hated your parents using, such as, 'Money doesn't grow on trees you know.'
- In this 'I want everything and I want it now!' era, children will quickly learn the hard knock lesson of life – we all know too well, you can't always have what you want.

Well, that all sounds very easy but in reality does it work, and how? To be honest, in the beginning they generally spend all their allowance in the first couple of days and then ask for more money for the bus to get to school, so to help your children make it work, sit down with them and discuss what they will have to buy from the money and how best to make it last and even to save for something. The amount of their allowance will obviously increase as they get older and become more independent.

First, work out how much they actually need, which may include transport to school and lunch money.

Then agree on what they will have to buy themselves and what you will still buy for them. Although you will have little say in their choice of clothes, this is an area where you should be in control of the purse strings, so do not include this expense in their allowance, although this does not mean a new item of clothing every week. The sort of items you and your children may wish to consider including in their budget are (depending on their age):

- CDs and DVDs
- Video rental, unless it's a film the whole family wants to watch
- Make-up (hopefully just for the girls)
- Magazines and books
- Confectionery and snacks
- Cinema tickets
- A fast food meal
- 'Pay as you go' mobile phone vouchers
- Drinks
- Entry to clubs
- Public transport
- Taxis (shared with friends)

These are simply items to be discussed, not included *every* week in their allowance. It is sometimes a good idea to talk to your children's friends' parents about how much allowance they are giving their children. Too little, for instance enough for their bus fare and a couple of packets of gum on top is too mean, but on the other hand, being given enough to go the cinema, buy a magazine, a cheap meal and a CD every week is far too generous. Make it a realistic amount and they are far more likely to live within it and learn something from it.

Although this may sound strange, decide with daughters how much a year you will allow them to have for the hairdressers and beauty salons (yes, from as young as fourteen girls use them for waxing, etc) and that way if they wish to have their hair highlighted, they must realize that they will not be able to afford the roots being re-touched every six to eight weeks.

What if They Run Out

If they run out they will probably ask for more, or an advance on the following week.

Quite simply, but firmly, say, 'No'. Explain that as an employee you couldn't go to the boss and say that you'd overspent this month and could you have some of next month's salary now. Don't let flattery sway you either: 'Oh, pleeeease, mum, you're the best, youngest, most beautiful mum in the world, and I promise it won't ever happen again.' Youngest, most beautiful? Okay, that does make it more tricky, but stand firm, you are doing your children an injustice if you give in, and there will be a next time, probably sooner than you could possibly imagine, because you will have just trained your children that if they run out of money, you'll give them more.

However, you could suggest that if they wanted to make some extra cash they could iron the entire contents of the washing basket or cook and clean up after supper or do some other job. One very important rule you must adhere to when allowing them to work for extra money, is that the job must be done before the cash is handed over. Explain to them that no one with a brain cell is going to pay them now for a chore they may do some time in the future.

For your own peace of mind stick to this rule otherwise you will end up feeling put upon and resentful. This is when comments such as, 'You treat me like a bank,' just cause bad feeling between parent and child and yet it's clear to see that sadly it is the parent's fault. If every time we went to the bank and asked the cashier for some money (which wasn't ours) and we were given it, with dubious chance of repayment, wouldn't we keep going back for more?

Depending on how well your children cope with their allowance, when they reach fifteen or sixteen you can start giving them their allowance on a monthly, rather than weekly basis, to see how they cope. If they start running out halfway through the month, put them back onto the more manageable weekly basis.

If they are desperate to borrow money for a certain item and you agree to lend it, be absolutely sure you get it back. You may even have to work out together just exactly how and when it will be repaid before you agree to the loan.

Separated Parents

Trying to teach your children to handle money can go awry if, when they visit their other parent they are given a whack of money. This money may be because the parent feels that they don't see their children that often or guilty because of the reasons for the separation.

If you are on speaking terms with your ex then explain about the allowance and suggest they either pay half or put money into a bank account for your children which can accumulate and go towards a car in the future. If you are not on speaking terms then write and explain, pointing out that it is for the benefit of the child.

If you notice children have suddenly got new clothes or CDs which you didn't give them the money for, ask where it came from. If it came from their other parent, on the odd occasion it happens say nothing, but if it starts to happen on a regular basis speak to your ex about it. Explain how it simply isn't the best thing for their child to be showered with clothes and gifts, so why not put the money into their savings account.

Grandparents

If your children's grandparents regularly give them money, again simply ask them to put that money into their savings account, as they are on allowance and it will only be squandered. If they only give them money occasionally, then just leave it and perhaps suggest to your children that they put it in their bank. Expect a quizzical 'Why?' look from your teens.

Bank Accounts

All children should have their own bank accounts from a young age, so that some birthday/Christmas/Easter money can be banked to accumulate for when they are older. As they become teenagers, avoid letting them have access to their own account if you feel the temptation of the saved money will be too great. As an alternative, move the saved money to a savings (with interest) account and pay their allowance into their current account by standing order so they can access it with a bank card.

part-time jobs

Part-time jobs are the best way for children to learn the value of money; after all, apart from the extra cash they will earn, the reality check of hard graft, long hours and poor pay for menial work should be the biggest incentive to get teenagers to work hard for better exam results if ever there was one.

Once they are sixteen, help your children find part-time work and suggest they draw up a CV (see page 93), to include their name, age, address, school, what they are studying, contact numbers and when they would be available to work. Make sure that your children are not taking on a part-time job which will take up too much of their time when they should be studying or revising.

They need to include a short personal statement to include why they will be suitable for the position; for instance, they are good with people, polite, punctual, honest and hard working. Ask a school teacher if they would write a short reference and attach a photocopy. Also tell your children to attach a passport-size photo, preferably smiling and looking straight at the camera. Looking shifty, covered in body piercings or wearing a three-inch layer of make-up may not be the best image for a future employer. But be diplomatic in the way you impart this information if you think your child falls into these images.

Whatever job your children are applying for, explain as best you can what the job will probably entail. For example, working in a clothes shop will mean being on their feet all day (so make sure they wear comfortable shoes and not their favourite three-inch heels), picking up clothes other people have dropped onto the changing room floors and putting them on hangers and, oh my god, they don't even know how to use a hanger! They should have their mobile phone turned off at all times and should ask beforehand if they should take a sandwich in or will they actually be able to leave the shop for their lunch-hour to get something to eat. Suggest your teenage daughter removes or replenishes nail varnish as chipped varnish is so unsightly. They must be happy to do whatever they are asked with a willingness and lack of attitude. But also explain that although they are only part-timers, they should be treated with respect from other employees and warn daughters to let you know if any members of staff or the public make suggestive or improper remarks to them. Remember, as they are in their first job, they are in a vulnerable position and, just because they are young and part-time, they should still be treated with respect.

As with all stages of their development, if they know exactly what is expected of them and what to expect they will feel far more confident. The one thing you can warn them about (but they will not believe it until they experience it), is how rude the general public can be.

And finally, the most important piece of advice all children (and some adults I know) should learn if they are going to do a job, whatever it is, however menial or boring: do the very best they can and to be polite, helpful and to smile at their customers.

> **Fran:** 'I had a part-time job in a clothes shop before Christmas and although I tried to be polite to all the customers, lots of them were really quite rude to me. I was the youngest working there and I felt that because I was a teenager, some adults just didn't feel it necessary to be nice to me. It's like we're stereotyped as rude and obnoxious, however we behave.'

school

Expectations

We all want our children to be successful and we all want to be proud of them, that's absolutely normal, but some parents are so determined that their children will succeed that they actually cause them more anxiety and stress than necessary, sometimes with fatal results.

Some parents are blinded by their own dreams and aspirations for their children and drive them towards goals, irrespective of the child's ambition. Very often it comes from parents who were unsuccessful at achieving exactly what they wanted as young adults and either want to live their dreams through their children or see them succeed where they failed. Whatever the reason, it is harmful and stressful for children. For example, because a child has a natural ability to kick a ball and the father is a huge Arsenal supporter, it doesn't necessarily follow that their son wants to be a professional footballer, even if his father wants it. Some parents take their children's lack of career decision as a sign that they must decide for them, and not simply that their child has yet to come to a decision.

But children who try and live up to their parent's unrealistic expectations, regardless of how realistic the parents believe them to be, will end up demoralized, overcome by a feeling of failure and sometimes depressed.

Parents can become angry and frustrated with their children when they realize that they are not going to live up to their dreams, succeed where they failed, or even be as successful as they were. Suddenly the dream is over: no professional footballers, famous QCs or Shakespearian actors, just travel agents and receptionists. As teenagers would say, 'Get over it, move on.'

Or just because a parent went to a certain university or belongs to a certain profession it does not necessarily mean it will be the right university or profession for their teen. A child from a family of doctors may not decide to follow the same path and sometimes parents do have issues with this, 'But the MacEnemas have been doctors for the past 70 years, what do you mean you want to be in advertising?' Part of growing up is about making their own decisions and although we must be there to help guide them we must certainly not try to control and seal their future fate. However, we can point out where their natural talents lie: maybe they are good with people, or artistic, or good with their hands, or have brilliant scientific minds, so they can make up their own minds.

If by the time they leave for university they still haven't decided what they want to do in the future, don't panic, it doesn't mean they are never going to have a successful, fulfilling career, it simply means they don't know what it is yet. At this point in their lives it is just as, if not more important to have confident, well-balanced, good-humoured, charming young adults who feel they have the world at their feet.

One way for teens to get an idea of what they might want to do is by working in different professions on unpaid work experience to get a feel for what they might like.

Pushy, Rude Parents on the Sports Field

There's little point trying to set a good example and teach children to respect their fellow man when parents turn up at school matches and are in such disagreement with the referee that they start swearing at them and the opposing team.

This simply teaches children that they can question and argue with authority, and that winning is everything.

Some of these parents will even encourage their children to cheat just as long as their team wins. Premiership football offers scant example for young sport enthusiasts, where foul play and diving are regularly seen and dealt with leniently. Surely swearing or arguing with the referee should be a sending off offence and, in my opinion, spitting would warrant a yellow card.

Anyone who takes part in a sport should try their hardest to win but not at the cost of their dignity, integrity and manners. Perhaps all parents who like to support their children's sports team would be wise to watch professional rugby: when the referee makes a decision the player stands non-aggressively with his hands behind his back and says, 'Yes, sir.' Now that's respect.

exams

Teenagers (and parents!) can become very stressed at the time of end of year exams, GCSEs and AS/A2 levels. There is so much pressure put on our children to succeed these days that they can easily become anxious and depressed.

First, remember, that although the media would have us believe that if you can write your name correctly you'll get an A grade, it is not quite that easy. Not all children are academics, just as not all children are naturally artistic or brilliant at sport. So don't pressurize them into thinking if they don't get straight As they have failed the entire family. Yes, we all want our children to do well, but at the end of the day, as long as they work hard and do their best, if the best they can do is a C then that's really the best they can do. And it should be rewarded. Never promise rewards just for good results; if your children have really worked hard, regardless of their results, they should get a reward.

Choosing Subjects

My daughter's headmistress told the assembled parents not to pack their children's lunch boxes for them, which was a metaphor for letting them choose their own A subjects, as they were the ones who were going to be learning them. I've always thought this a very sensible piece of advice. Parents, teachers and career advisers can all offer advice but it must be your teen who makes the final decision; after all they are the ones who will have to sit through two years of tuition.

Coursework and Revision

Not unlike a mounting basket of ironing, revision and coursework can be put off and put off until the very thought of it is too overwhelming to even begin. So just

87

like the saying, 'How do you eat an elephant?' the answer being, 'A mouthful at a time,' suggest that teenagers take this approach to their work (and the ironing!). Teenagers are not very good at time management and coursework is one area which often gets left until almost too late. Coursework marks are the easiest marks to achieve as pupils have input from their teachers. And starting with a good coursework grade makes getting a good overall grade that much more attainable.

Ask if you can help them organize a revision timetable, so they know exactly what they are doing. For example, from 9.30am to 10.15am revise English, then have a fifteen minute break and then geography, etc. While they are revising, keep them going with nourishing tasty snacks and drinks and words of encouragement. Make sure they take breaks from their work and get a good night's sleep. Always encourage them to tell you if they have any problems or if there is any part of their work that they don't understand – not that I'm suggesting you will be able to help directly, but you can call up the school for advice about what to do.

Words of motivation such as, 'Just think, in two months you'll never have to pick up another biology book again,' or empathy, as in 'I don't blame you for being fed-up, no one likes exams darling, so you may as well just buckle down and get them over with. You'll only be letting yourself down if you don't work at them.'

Some children concentrate better if there is background sound, so don't think you know best when you tell them to turn off their music, as long as it's not too loud, but you do know best when you tell them to turn off the

'Billy, are you revising?' 'Yes, mum.'

TV, as it's far too visual, no phone calls or texting, and the internet is for work only, no chat lines or games.

If they are really having difficulty, suggest they ease themselves into their revision with just ten minutes work then a break, then another ten minutes and another break, gradually building up the time they are actually working to twenty, thirty, forty minutes at a time between breaks. If you have the time (try and find it), ask if you can test them on what they have been revising. It relieves the monotony of working alone, but remember to be encouraging, avoiding comments such as, 'Well, I don't know what you've been doing for the past hour, 'cause you certainly don't know anything about photosynthesis,' and replacing them with constructive comments like, 'You're doing well darling, but there are a few gaps, so let's go over those parts again.'

Mind Mapping

One revision tool that your children will find really useful is a Mind Map®. Mind Mapping is a unique system of note-taking and planning that engages both sides of the brain for maximum mental agility. This is because you draw them with colours and images as well as words. (More traditional, mono-coloured and linear note-taking methods only engage the left side of the brain, making it immediately more difficult to remember information.)

MIND MAPS ARE PARTICULARLY HELPFUL WHEN IT COMES TO:

- **Organizing information.** Mind Maps will help your children to see links between information and to sort out and group facts in a coherent, memorable way.
- **Summing up information.** With a Mind Map it is easy to sum up all the information on a single page instead of on several pieces of paper. This gives your children immediate confidence and a greater sense of control.
- **Planning revision.** A revision Mind Map will give your children an excellent overview of which subjects they need to revise and when – this is particularly effective if your children's time management skills are chaotic.
- **Remembering information.** Because they engage the full power of both sides of the brain, Mind Maps are much easier to learn from than conventional notes.
- **Enjoying learning.** Because Mind Maps are actually quite fun – and relaxing – to draw, your children should find the whole revision process less arduous.

For more information on Mind Mapping and handy memory and revision tips, see *Mind Maps for Kids: Max Your Memory and Concentration* or *Mind Maps for Kids: Rev Up for Revision* by the Mind Map genius, Tony Buzan.

Exam Days

Get your children off to a good start with a protein breakfast such as a boiled egg or egg and grilled bacon with a piece of wholemeal toast. Avoid the sugary cereals and white toast, as this will make their brains sluggish and that's the last thing they want. Give them an encouraging pep talk, telling them that they know they can do it, you're really proud of how hard they have worked, and if there are questions they can't do, then too bad, it doesn't mean they're not going to be superstars when they leave school and have a life of misery, it just means they couldn't answer a question. Give them a big hug and tell them how much you love them and wish them luck. Suggest they get to school a bit earlier, if possible, so they have time for a quick run around to oxygenate their brain and kick start it. Recent research has shown that physical exercise increases cerebral blood flow and spurs brain cell growth (that's got to help, hasn't it?). Exercise also has positive effects on mood, so basically you will feel better after exercise even though you are about to sit a major exam.

> **Katherine:** 'When I get home after an exam I hate it when my parents ask how it went. I know they only mean well but when I've just sat through three hours on some subject, I want to forget it, there is nothing I or they can do about it now, a post-mortem won't help my results.'

The Results

Not everyone is going to get the grades they want. Some children will be terribly upset by their results, so don't make comments such as, 'Well, I told you you should have worked harder,' or 'Don't tell me you're surprised, you've only got yourself to blame.' Try a little sympathy, after all, their punishment is their poor grades, and the last thing they need is a parent smugly reiterating, 'I told you so.' Stay calm, don't shout, and when everyone has had time to digest the disappointing news, sit down and talk it through.

If they've passed, celebrate, tell them how proud you are. If you have two children, one with great grades and one who is disappointed, be diplomatic. Explain to the successful child in private why you can't make a big fuss of them in front of their sibling, but emphasize how proud and delighted you are for them.

If your child didn't receive the results they needed to get to their chosen university, they will be devastated. You probably will be too, but don't show it, sit them down and talk through what you will do next. Life doesn't finish because of less than perfect grades. As Mark Twain said, 'I never let my schooling interfere with my education.'

> **Sam:** 'Every person my age, whatever attitude they give off, is worried what their parents think about their results, so whatever the results are, always be supportive and reassure them how proud you are of them.'

work

Curriculum Vitae

Curriculum vitae is Latin for 'the course of one's life' and the very first thing to note is most employers will quickly bin any CV that has the words 'curriculum vitae' spelt incorrectly (and they receive them by the skipful!).

A CV is your teenager's advertisement to future employers. It is used when applying for an advertised job or if they are enquiring about positions available. Employers can receive hundreds of CVs, so it is important that your child's CV is interesting, factual and stands out.

Some dos and don'ts of preparing a good CV:

- Construct on a word-processor or type.
- Use no more than two fonts or print sizes.
- Be generous with borders and white spaces to create easy reading.

- Use a straightforward, simple layout.
- Try and keep it to one A4 sheet (this should be easy as they will not have had much if any previous work experience).
- Good spelling and grammar are essential.
- Read and re-read it and ask a teacher or another parent to look over the CV before finalizing it.
- Include personal details, such as name and address, date of birth, phone number and email address. If they include a photo make sure it's a good one, not one taken by their friends when they are three sheets to the wind or when they were experimenting with facial piercings and pink hair.

Ciriculom Vitay

NAME: Sam Palmano
AGE : 18 (but have I.D for 21)
SEX: Every night
EXPERIENCE: Lots. As I said, every night (see SEX)

REFERENCES: Tracey
Sandra
Vickay
Tracey's sister

- List education and qualifications with no exaggerations, concentrating on GCSE and above. Duke of Edinburgh awards and any awards that may show dedication, team work or leadership qualities should be included.
- List other qualifications such as a clean driving licence, foreign languages or computer skills.
- Give a brief synopsis of any previous work experience such as Saturday jobs or paper rounds (list the most recent first and give dates).
- Include interests such as sports or hobbies.
- A short personal synopsis pointing out their qualities is essential, for example, good with people, punctual, responsible, etc.
- Give names, addresses and contact numbers of two references, for example, teachers, or friends of the family who have known them for a long time. Make sure they are willing to give a reference.
- Send a CV with a covering letter personalized for the particular company they are applying to, and make sure they telephone first to get the name of the person they should address it to.

Interviews

Whether your teenager has decided to go to university or some other higher or vocational training, or requires a part- or full-time job, they may well be required to go for an interview, and the way they present themselves during the interview can make the difference between being offered the position or not.

Amazingly (shockingly), this is a true story. The owner of an electronics business who was interviewing for an apprentice said that, as he was talking to one teenage applicant, he could hear a buzzing noise. He realized that the teenager had not turned off his iPod; in fact he was listening to it during the interview. Needless to say he didn't get the job, which was given to a teenager who turned up wearing a suit. As the owner remarked, 'If he makes the effort to wear a suit to the interview, he just might make the effort if he works for me.'

Most schools will teach some interviewing skills, but here's a list of dos and don'ts to help prepare your children. They should:

- Dress smartly – it's best to get their clothes ready the night before, rather than panic on the day when their best shirt is found on the floor with ketchup stains all over it.
- Find out information on the company/shop/college and think up some relevant questions they want to ask.
- Make sure they have pre-prepared some answers to questions that will likely be asked.
- Be on time, in fact a few minutes early. It is inexcusable to be late for an interview, so get them to find out exactly where it is they are going and how long it will take to get there.
- Take their CV with them even if they've already sent it.

- Know the name of the person who will conduct the interview and exactly how it is pronounced.
- Walk up to the interviewer, give a firm handshake, look them directly in the eye as they say, 'Good morning, Mr Jones,' and introduce themselves. Remember to smile, it is so important.
- Sit upright, poised but confident (however they may really feel).
- Listen to what is being said and answer in full sentences (not in monosyllables), but avoid rambling. Always look the interviewer in the eye.
- Look interested and enthusiastic and ask appropriate questions about the job or course.
- Don't smoke, even if offered one, and don't chew gum.
- Make sure that they get across their good points.
- Be honest – if they know they will not be able to work Saturday afternoons because of sport commitments, it is best to be upfront and explain.
- Answer questions honestly and frankly.
- Thank the interviewer for his or her time.

To help prepare them, suggest they ask a teacher or relative to give them a mock interview or offer to do so at home, but don't be surprised or offended if they refuse.

five

Communication

Communication is one of the most important factors in keeping good relations with your teenagers. And there are three components to communication which are imperative: empathizing, listening and honesty.

The easiest way to keep track of your growing children is by being involved in their day-to-day lives. This is not to say you interrupt or listen in to their phone calls, or read their diaries and private notes, but it is about keeping the lines of communication open at all times and taking time out to talk to them. You're probably wondering how on earth you do that when they come home from school, leave their shoes and everything else they were carrying right inside the front door and disappear to their room to watch TV or get onto their computer until they go to bed.

how to talk to teenagers

Not unlike toddlers (but never mention this to them), teenagers are desperate for independence and, just as with toddlers, the more responsibility you give them the happier they will be.

First, try and empathize with how your teenager thinks. Imagine four people being given an ink blot and being asked to describe what the image reminds them of. No doubt each person will give a different account of what they see, because we all see things differently. So your teenager will see the world and issues differently to the way we see it. In fact, it would be very boring if our children had exactly the same views as us about absolutely everything. We want individuals, not clones. And now is the time to encourage their opinions, not suppress them or try and tell them what they should think.

Secondly, lines of communication will only remain open if you can listen, without constantly interrupting and being non-judgemental. And thirdly, be honest. If there is an issue you are worried about or that needs settling, be honest and tell your teenager. They are very quick to condemn hypocrites and are much more likely to be honest with you if they know you are honest with them.

Once your teenager realizes that you will listen and you do take them seriously, they will be much more receptive and willing to talk and discuss with you. Be a parent who is always prepared to listen but not one who always has all the answers.

Finally, finding the time to talk can be difficult, what with longer school hours, after-school activities, going out and spending time on the phone and computer, so the very easiest way to guarantee time is to eat around the table in the evening.

Apart from talking directly to your teenagers, they will also learn from discussion about current news events your thoughts and opinions on a whole range of issues from drug-taking to joy-riding.

Supper together is probably the only time you will get to really talk every day.

Now your children are older and not expected to be in bed by 8pm, there is no reason why you cannot all eat together every evening. No one is expecting gourmet meals, just something easy and healthy; you can even have a takeaway occasionally. Now they are teenagers this time around the table is invaluable for many reasons.

- It's the only time during the day when you can all talk together.
- You can supervise what they eating (especially daughters).
- You will notice any change in their moods or behaviour.
- You will detect any problems or anxieties they may have.
- They will still be learning from your example.
- You can discuss any general problems – more personal problems should be discussed on a one-to-one basis in private.

Teenagers seldom want to talk about their school day or how their work is going, so talk about their interests or bring up an issue that's in the news and relevant to them. Music, fashion, films, TV, celebrities in the media and everyday dilemmas are good subjects and easy for teenagers to join in with their opinions.

Remember to listen to their opinions and express an interest in what they are saying. Don't immediately tell them they don't know what they're talking about because you don't happen to agree. Keep personal issues away from the table or the conversation will quickly collapse into an argument with your teenager storming off. Whatever jokes or one-liners they crack about their parents, they take a very dim view of anyone trying to take the mickey out of them. Adolescence is a very sensitive time, so avoid humiliating or embarrassing them and instead say something encouraging or flattering. And finally, always try and have a laugh, as laughter relieves stress and is very bonding for the entire family.

If you've all had a good time at supper, suggest you all stay at the table and play something like cards or 'What's in the bag?'

GUIDELINES FOR FAMILY MEALS

- Absolutely no mobile phones at the table. Anyone calling on a home line will be asked to call back later.
- Any arguments with siblings are not brought to the table.
- No TV on.
- Don't bring up anything that is likely to be controversial, for example, they are not going out on Saturday night unless their room is tidy.
- Don't embarrass anyone at the table with comments about their friends, relationships, hair or clothes, etc.

If there are younger siblings at the table, let them get down after supper and then continue talking about more adult subjects with your teenagers. If you have had a good time with them, thank them for their good company.

> **Sam:** 'We always try and eat a few nights a week around the table. It's good just to talk and have a laugh and my sisters and I love to rinse* our parents.'

breakdown in communication

You are not alone if you feel you have had a complete breakdown in communications with your teenager. There are literally hundreds of thousands of parents this happens to, but the good news is, it is repairable.

It could be sparked by an argument or just caused by gradual erosion. With the busy lives we all lead, it is very easy to put off supper around the table, so your teenagers eat alone off a tray in front of the TV or in their room. With everyone rushing in and out to get to work and school, conversation gets bypassed in favour of orders and questions, 'It's time to get up for school,' 'Put your cereal bowl in the sink,' 'Good day at school?' 'Supper's ready,' 'Don't shout at your brother!' 'How much longer are you going to be in that bathroom?' 'Have you done your homework?' 'Goodnight.'

Over time, even a short period, this lack of communication and family closeness gets further and further strained, you talk less, touch less, until there is an issue which explodes into an argument with shouting on both sides. Often, from then on it's a matter of the teenager rebelling against the parent's every wishes, even to the

* See Glossary, page 255.

point of leaving the house and slamming the door behind them when spoken to.

Repairing the Damage

With a breakdown of communication there is also a breakdown of respect and the way you handle this situation will not only get you and your teen back on track but it will also teach your teenager the valuable lesson of mending bridges. As the parent you will be the one who has to make the first move. First, if you have shouted at them, go and quietly apologize without adding that they deserved it or drove you to it, and ask them to come and talk to you. Make sure there are no nosy siblings around to interfere.

Sit opposite each other and calmly talk through any issues and listen to what your teenager has to say. If the breakdown has been caused by an argument over some issue, see if there is a way of compromising. Note that this does not mean parents giving in, but perhaps both parties could budge slightly to come to an agreement.

Start eating as a family around a table in the evenings without the TV on and start talking and laughing as a family together. And don't forget how important physical contact is: hugs, a cuddle, sitting with your arms around them are all reassuring, supportive gestures and tell them you love them.

If you've had a row and it's degenerated into name-calling, however hurt you are, you are the parent, you must offer the olive branch, so if you can't speak to them, send a text, such as 'sorry we argued luv u mum xx'.

mother and daughter relationships

There is no relationship quite like that of mother and daughter. From a very young age daughters see their

mums as goddesses: not only do they want to constantly be with them and play with them but they want to be like them, with high heels, lipstick-covered faces, dressing-up and jewellery. Little girls smother their mummies with love and cuddles so what could possibly go wrong? Oops! Come thirteen and suddenly the goddess is now old-fashioned, ignorant, stupid, uncool and lucky to get five minutes of their daughter's invaluable time.

Even in the warmest and closest of families, mother and daughter relationships can be become strained and acrimonious. Some psychologists suggest it is because mothers find it hard to accept their daughters as adult, but whatever the reason it can lead to some conflict-ridden exchanges. Teenage girls are often closer to their fathers during adolescence.

When a daughter reaches her teens she has to push her mother away in order to make the separation and prepare for her independence. Girls will often be quite verbal during this separation process, which is very upsetting for mothers. It's not that unusual in some families for daughters to scream, 'I hate you!' at their mothers, and even if this happens to you, don't worry, she doesn't really hate you. Some mothers often complain they can't even be in the same room with their daughter without sparks flying.

The good news is that once daughters are in their twenties the relationship with their mothers usually settles down, but do try and avoid too much upset during their teens – try and follow a few guidelines.

Treat her as the young adult she is becoming, let her know that you trust her to do the right thing and more often than not she will. Constantly trying to get her to do everything you want and adopt your views will end up with you both at each other's throats.

Every time your daughter says something which you disagree with or you feel is being said to taunt and provoke you, take a deep breath and think before engaging your mouth. Encourage her to talk about her friends (but never push on the new boyfriend front) and be complimentary about them. The quickest way to alienate your daughter, or son, is to constantly criticize their friends. Take the time to do some girlie things with your daughter. Let her choose a film and go to the cinema together, or take her and a friend out to lunch. If your daughter has a special party to go to, offer to treat her to a hairdo or a manicure.

Always listen to what she says and don't expect her to accept your point of view, as at the end of the day it's only your view.

Pay her compliments about how she looks – no woman wants to spend two hours getting ready only for someone to look at them and criticize their appearance.

And don't forget to tell her that you love her and show her you love her by giving her a hug and doing kind things for her, even though she is totally wrapped up in herself (it's her age). Don't take the attitude, 'Well, why should I do anything nice for her, when she doesn't do anything for me?' Remember, you are the mother and your daughter is going through puberty – you are the adult and she is still half child.

As we're all human, if or when it all goes belly up and you end up shouting, even though you believe it was your daughter in the wrong, you're the mother, the example, the adult, so apologize, and say, 'I'm sorry I shouted.'

Show your daughter respect and she is far more likely to show you respect.

Don't Try and Be 'Best Friends'

Mothers who insist they are best friends with their teenage daughters are, in my opinion, a bit sad. Girls discuss everything with their best friends, but especially boys, sex, friends, boys, innermost thoughts, worries, hopes and boys. Surely daughters should not be discussing all those topics with their mother in the depth they are going to confide in friends. Friends fulfil, quite rightly, a different agenda to that of a parent.

I would be horrified if I told my mother half the things I used to discuss with my best friend at that age (and so would she). Mothers should also have their best friends to chat and confide in, but these certainly shouldn't be their teenage daughters.

Mothers and teenage daughters can have a wonderful, warm, loving close relationship, but it should always be mother and daughter and not 'best friends'. Mothers who insist they borrow each other's clothes and go out drinking and pulling together need to get a life of their own, and let their daughters start to lead their own lives with their own friends. Mothers should be there for support and guidance, not to decide where they are both going clubbing together. Regardless of how much teens bemoan the fact that they have curfews and boundaries, they are in fact much happier for it and feel reassured of being loved and cared for. They will feel more secure knowing exactly what the relationship is.

Daughters have all sorts of issues of their own, and what they need is a loving, supportive mother, not one who has needs of her own to be filled by their daughter.

divorce

Divorce is an extremely difficult and traumatic experience for everyone. Statistics show that 28 per cent of all children under sixteen years old will experience their parents' separation. For teenagers going through their own emotional roller-coaster of hormones and mood swings, it is particularly difficult. They are just at an age where they are working out where they belong in the world and their only real stability, the framework in which they have developed, is suddenly collapsing. They see their parents upset, angry and, even worse, needy. They will experience feelings of anger, confusion, worry, fear and even thoughts that it may be their fault. They can also feel resentful towards their parents, as if to say, 'Look, you should be concentrating on my problems, not yours.'

However traumatized, bitter or upset parents are they must talk honestly to their teens. Screaming and shouting behind closed doors and living in an atmosphere you can cut with a knife is not something you can hide from children, so it's much better to sit down and explain what is happening and, above all, that none of this is their fault. It is unlikely that both parents will be able to sit at the same time with their teens to discuss what is happening without one parent or the other making snide comments about whose fault it is and the 'discussion' rapidly plummeting into a full-blown row.

Children will and should feel great loyalty to both parents, so however angry or bitter you feel, avoid discrediting and basically slagging off their other parent in front of them. This will only make them feel more confused as to where their loyalties should lie. Explain what is going to happen, don't try and hedge issues. Your teens will need to know where they will be living and with whom, whether the house will be sold, where the other parent (usually the father) will be living, who they will spend the holidays and Christmas with. Mothers – do not try and limit the amount of time they can see their father; they have lived with him for the past 13 to 16 years, so why should they not be able to see him whenever they like. Don't fuel your battles by using your children as ammunition. If you can't bring yourself to speak to your ex, then text, email or write but never use your children as go-betweens to take messages or ask questions from one to the other.

Encourage your children to ask questions about the new situation and answer them truthfully and directly without discrediting anyone (new partners, for example).

Keep telling them how much you both love your children and although you don't want to live together anymore they are free to go between both parents whenever they want.

Organize an adult, maybe a good friend, a god-parent, uncle or teacher who your teens like and trust, to talk to them about the situation. Sometimes children may well say things that are on their mind to trusted friends rather than to parents. And they need someone outside of the immediate family to be able to confide in and talk to.

single parents

Single parenting a teenager is tough. To be honest, it's probably harder for the parent than the child. The teenager will do what teenagers do and disappear into their room, phone their friends or play on their computer, leaving the parent sitting alone downstairs, quite often feeling resentful and lonely.

The main problem with single parenting is the lack of back-up. When issues or arguments arise there is no one else to talk it over with, to help you to decide on strategy or simply to sit down with a glass of wine and discuss the situation.

If a teenager is seeing both parents, less conflict will be caused if the same rules are implemented in both households, for instance, if the mother insists on her son being back at eleven but the father lets him stay out until one, problems are bound to arise. Parents on talking terms should reconcile to treat their child the same in both homes, but if talking is not an option, then one parent should write to the other explaining the situation and how much better it would be for their child if they agreed on certain principles.

In other situations, if for instance an argument has flared, the teenager can announce that they are going to live with the other parent and sometimes do, but do not let them start coming and going every time they don't get their own way. This is very unsatisfactory for both parents and just teaches teenagers that they can run away from problems. Parents should each (or, if possible both) sit down with their teenager to discuss the situation and agree that their time may be split between the two homes, but at arranged times, and not just when they disagree about something with one parent.

Teenagers need to learn how to negotiate and compromise, not simply run to one parent when things are not going all their own way.

A single mother with a teenage boy who does not see his father very often, if at all, needs to get a male role model involved in her son's life – someone he can look up to and learn from.

The plus side to being a single parent is that when the children go to stay with the other parent it allows time to recharge the parental batteries.

step-parents

The merging of two families is always going to bring a myriad of problems with it, which only time, patience, understanding and consideration can improve and yes, it is possible that step-families can live in harmony.

Although two adults from different families may have fallen madly in love and want to spend the rest of their lives in marital bliss, it does not necessarily mean that any of the children involved will embrace the idea of a step-family.

The younger the children, the easier it is, but by the time children are in their teens life will certainly become more challenging. A teenage boy of one family may not be particularly overjoyed at having a nine-year-old step-brother who continually follows him around and pokes around in his room. Children are not going to be delighted that a step-parent is coming to live in the home they used to share with both parents, or perhaps it will suddenly seem over-crowded if there are now three people when there were only two.

Children have loyalties to both parents, regardless of who broke up with who and why. So they can feel very disloyal in showing emotion to a new step-parent, and often resent the fact that their step-parent is not only sharing their home but also their mother or father. At this crucial age, teenagers often take umbrage at being told what to do or disciplined by a step-parent. They do not like the way family celebrations have to be compromised or how 'things have changed'. They may be jealous of how their mother is showering her new partner and step-daughter with affection. Children can feel that their father prefers to be with his new step-children than with them, and so it goes on.

But careful handling, understanding and reassurance can help create a new happy family.

Steps to smooth the way for step-parents:

• Sit down and explain to your children exactly what is happening. Your children will need to know where they are going to live, and which room their new step-siblings will sleep in. Many children will not take kindly to having to share their room or seeing their new step-father in their father's bed or father's chair. If possible, move to a different property which is neutral to everyone and indicates a new start. Family homes are too fuelled with emotion and memories.

- Discuss with your new partner the way in which you will treat and discipline your new family, treating all the children the same. Parents must support each other. When possible the biological parent should discipline their own children, especially teens, to avoid the shouting, 'You can't tell me what to do, you're not my real father.'
- Don't try and be the mother or father of a step-teen. Take them out for a meal and discuss how things can work for both of you and the other members of the family.
- Step-parents are more likely to earn the respect of their step-teen if they are friendly and understanding and not immediately trying to replace their biological parent.
- Teens are having a tough emotional time with their own hormones so don't expect instant love or affection. Some step-parents and step-children may never even like each other.
- Step-parents of younger children (who are unaccustomed to the charms of teenagers) may immediately feel resentment at the way the new step-teen takes his natural parent for granted and spends most of the day in front of the TV.
- If teenagers are actively involved in sport or a certain interest, keep them involved.
- Encourage step-children to talk about their other parent or perhaps what they did with them at the weekend and never, ever criticize them.
- Be understanding when step-siblings don't get on. Just because the adults love each other doesn't mean the

children have to, but they do have to show a certain respect for each other.

- If, as a step-parent, you can see your step-children are depressed or worried, take them aside and quietly and calmly try to get them to say why. Let them realize that you are someone they can talk to and trust.
- Don't try and buy their affection with gratuitous presents or cash hand-outs.
- When things are going wrong and tempers flare, don't take on all the responsibility and guilt. Everyone in the home is involved, new relationships take time, talking and compromising will always help.

Adjusting to new relationships takes time, not only to get used to the new arrangements but also to get used to the loss of their former family life.

good manners and behaviour

six

Table Manners

The object of table manners is not to demonstrate the most sophisticated knowledge of table etiquette, but to behave with a certain poise and graciousness and to use knives, forks and spoons efficiently with ease and confidence. Let's face it, appalling table manners don't only put other people off eating their meal but also put them off the perpetrator, which would be a huge shame if it is the girl of your son's dreams.

It won't be long until they are eating out with their friends and their boy/girlfriends or, even more terrifying, the parents of their boy/girlfriends. Never let your teenagers underestimate the value adults put on good manners. Rightly or wrongly, table manners can be perceived as speaking volumes about a person's upbringings and values.

Fran: 'It isn't just adults that notice bad table manners. I went out to eat with my boyfriend a few months ago and was actually disgusted by the way he was eating. It isn't the most attractive sight to see the boy you like with a half-chewed up pizza in his mouth, which is unintentionally being spat at you across the table when he's attempting to speak with his mouth full. (Understandably I think) it really put me off him!'

eating at home

This is mentioned many times throughout the book, but it simply can't be reiterated enough that the best (sometimes only) time you might get to actually talk to your teens and other children is around the supper table. Even if it's only three or four times a week and even if it's only a take-away supper it will be invaluable time spent with them.

You may well find that when your children (who had fairly good table manners) become teenagers their manners all go a bit awry. The way they suddenly start holding their knives and forks can be a bit novel, as can their being slouched all over the table. Don't bother barking at them; just a few gentle hints and reminders should put them back on the right track. It's more important that they are at the table talking to you than expressing the finest table etiquette. Obviously both would be great, but in the immortal words from that great classic film *Now Voyager*, 'Let's not ask for the stars, when we have the moon.'

However, during the time they are with you at the table, the following gentle reminders would be recommended.

- Sit upright and squarely on the chair, as teenagers are inclined to slump and put one knee up.
- Put napkins on their laps, or tuck them into their collar, if they are about to eat something like spaghetti, which is likely to slop over their favourite white top.
- There's elbows and elbows. Elbows resting on the edge of the table are fine, it's the elbows and arms all over the table that should be stopped.
- It really isn't necessary for teenagers to constantly fiddle with knives and forks or the salt and pepper.
- Wait until everyone has their food before starting to eat, unless told otherwise.
- Eat with mouths shut and don't talk with mouths full.
- Not to drink while they have food in their mouth, or slurp their drink.
- Put butter (jam, etc) onto their side plate before putting it on their bread.
- Break off a piece of bread roll as they want to eat it, not eating it as a whole or half.
- When they sit down, offer the basket of bread to ladies or guests first before helping themelves.
- Ask for things to be passed to them, rather than lean across someone or across the table.
- Never point at people or gesticulate with their knife or fork.
- Never eat off the knife, always the fork.
- Never hold the knife like a pen.
- Never turn the fork round and use it like a shovel.

- Not to put huge amounts into their mouths in one go, so they have to struggle to chew.
- Put their knife and fork down occasionally (prongs facing down), while they chew their food.
- If they are helping themselves to some more potatoes, for example, and there are two left, not to take both without asking who else would like one.
- When finished, put their knife and fork together, straight down the middle of the plate.
- Put their used napkin on their side plate.
- Thank the cook for the meal.
- Remember to compliment the cook on all or part of the meal (if the meat was like the sole of a boot, perhaps comment on the great roast potatoes).
- Replace 'Please may I get down,' with 'Do you mind if we go?' now they are teenagers.
- Always hold knives (or sharp utensils) handle first.
- Help clear the plates.

Although they should know how to eat correctly by now, if you have to remind them, rather than the order, 'Don't eat with …' try the slightly more cajoling, 'Remember to eat with …'

Clearing Up

As they get older, teach them how to wash up and dry, including saucepans, put food away, clear and wipe down kitchen surfaces. Clearing up can be accomplished very quickly if everyone gives a hand, so make sure they all help.

The more you get your children to contribute to the household, the more they will expect to do it. However, if you suddenly start asking your teenager to lay the table or wash up, with no previous 'helping' experience, be prepared to be confronted with a distorted, bewildered expression accompanied by an incredulous grunt of, 'Wot?'

Stay calm and explain that from now on they are going to contribute to the housework. It is never too late for them to start helping, although you will have to guide them through their first few attempts. Anything not washed up well enough goes back for them to do again. Rather than starting a monologue about why they should help more around the house (because it may be your fault for never making them as they grew up), talk about current events or films. Again this can be good talk time with children, whatever age. Of course, if you have more than one teenager, once they know what to do, they can do it together without your help, and remember if they don't finish it off properly, for instance by wiping down the work surfaces and around the sink, back they go. One day they may just thank you for making them do a job properly. One day. I wouldn't hold your breath.

how to behave in a restaurant

By the time they are teenagers, hopefully you can visit a restaurant in the knowledge that they are not going to throw tantrums and run around as soon as they've eaten.

But there are still a few reminders they may need to help the evening run smoothly and although you are obviously not going to read this list to them, be aware of them and quietly mention them if and when necessary.

- Try and keep voices down.
- Decide who is going to sit where and opposite whom before you go in, and reiterate that there will be no change of seating plan once in the restaurant.
- Say, 'Good evening,' to the waiter/waitress, looking them in the eye.
- Thank the person who takes their coat.
- Try not to fiddle with their knife and fork, and not to play with the salt, pepper or sugar.
- Look the waiter/waitress in the eye when ordering, and say 'Please'.
- Pull off a piece of bread to eat, don't take a bite out of a whole piece.
- Decide before you go to the restaurant whether the teenagers are going to be allowed a beer or wine (mixed with water) and let them know, so there is no arguing once there.
- Ask for the butter, etc to be passed, don't just lean across to get it.
- Sit straight and upright, not resting their head in their hands or on the table.
- Turn all mobile phones off, and no texting at the table.
- Wait until everyone has their meal before they start.
- Remember to say, 'Please', and 'Thank you'.
- Don't raise any issues that are likely to cause sulking or arguing.
- Talk to your teenagers but not about school.

- If at the end of the meal they've been great company, tell and thank them.

formal restaurants and dinners

Once they reach sixteen they may well be invited to more formal occasions, like a friend's sister's eighteenth birthday, a family wedding, or a smart restaurant with friend's parents.

Explain to boys that there are a few courtesies that will certainly get them noticed and labelled so polite and so well-mannered, the sort of reputation that can go a long way with girls and their parents (not to be sniffed at). For some reason, parents who perceive their daughter's boyfriend as very polite and well-mannered are usually less strict about curfews. First, remind boys to open doors and to remember the 'ladies first' rule and, if no waiter is in evidence, to help with their coats. To really impress at the table, the men should pull the chairs out for the ladies to sit down and finally, a courtesy which is seldom practised and is only relevant at tables of eight or less, if a lady gets up from the table for whatever reason, the men stand up until she leaves the table and again when she returns.

When they are faced with a series of knives and forks on each side of the plate, they should start at the outside and work their way to the centre with each course (if they've seen the film *Pretty Woman*, remind them of the way Julia Roberts was taught by the hotel manager). They should always wait until everyone at their table has been served before they start to eat.

Once every one is ready to leave the men should help the ladies from their seats and with their coats. On leaving the restaurant boys should thank and shake hands with the parents and if appropriate kiss the mother on the cheek.

Although if you mention this to your teenager he may well roll his eyes, look confused and say, 'Get serious.' The attention and praise that will be bestowed upon them will spur them on to repeat the performance the next time.

Some Special Circumstances

Some foods require a special way of eating them, so instead of the embarrassment of wondering what to do, here's what to tell them.

Mussels (for example, moules marinières) – Show your children how to remove one mussel from its shell and then use the empty shell as 'pincers', then remove one mussel at a time from its shell with the pincers, discard the empty shell onto a different plate and eat the mussel. Finally, they eat the remaining soup. Alternatively, shell the mussels into the soup and then eat.

String-type pasta (spaghetti, linguine, etc) – They should hold the fork in their right hand and a dessertspoon in their left (just like for desserts but the other way round) and take a few strands of the pasta. Then, putting their fork in the spoon, start to turn the fork to roll up the pasta. The spoon will aid the rolling process, hopefully ending up with a manageable mouthful. The secret is not to start rolling too many strands.

Asparagus – Eat asparagus by taking one at a time between their thumb and first two fingers of their right hand. The end they are holding is usually not eaten as it can be too woody. Dip the tip in the sauce and eat.

Globe artichokes – Pull off the leaves one at a time, dip in a sauce if appropriate and suck the 'flesh' from the blunt end. When all the leaves have been pulled off, use a knife and fork to cut away the 'hairy bit' and eat the heart.

> I remember attending a twenty-first birthday dinner when I was about seventeen and being confronted with a globe artichoke as a first course and having absolutely no idea how to tackle it. Surreptitiously, I glanced at my fellow diners who, I was relieved to see, were in an equal quandary. Fortunately, someone saw the host pulling off the leaves and we all started as though we'd known all along.

Wine

Help your teenagers to show a respect for wine and other alcoholic drinks by explaining their different qualities and properties. Explain which wines you would usually drink with different foods, keep it simple as white with fish and red with meat.

Explain and demonstrate how to correctly open a bottle of wine – if you don't show them correctly they might do as so many do and twist the bottle rather than the corkscrew.

The more social skills teenagers have the more confidence they will feel in different situations. (And personally, I think knowing how to open a bottle of wine or champagne correctly is a very necessary social skill.)

WINE GLASSES

We all know that teenagers (and us in moments of dire need) would happily drink directly from a plastic wine box, however, given the remote chance that they might be in a situation where they need to know, it's best they know the correct alternatives.

So while they are learning, they may as well learn correctly.

There are three main types of wine glasses:

- **Sparkling wine or champagne** – tall and thin flutes
- **White wine** – tulip shaped, or a smaller version of the red wine glass
- **Red wine** – usually larger, and more rounded with a larger bowl.

Explain that the shape of a wine glass can impact the taste of a good wine, something they probably won't have to worry about for some considerable time.

SERVING STILL WINE

Without getting too detailed, explain that as a general rule of thumb white and rosé wines should be served chilled while most red wines are served at room temperature.

To serve, the wine bottle should be held near the base of the bottle between the thumb and fingers. The bottle should not touch the glass and the wine should be poured into the centre of the glass and never more than two-thirds full, usually to the widest part of the glass. When the glass is sufficiently filled, the bottle should be twisted slightly to prevent drips.

At the table, wine should be served to women and older guests first, the pourer serving himself last.

OPENING SPARKLING WINES AND CHAMPAGNE

We've all seen the winners on the Formula One podium shaking up a magnum of champagne and spraying the crowd with it, but in the event your teenagers haven't won a Grand Prix, it's best to show your teenagers the correct way so that not a drop is wasted.

Too good to waste!

- Chill the bottle for about three hours in the refrigerator or half an hour in a bucket of iced water.
- Remove the foil over the cork.
- Untwist the wire mesh, usually 6 turns, and remove.
- Hold the cork firmly with one hand and the base of the bottle in the other at a 45-degree angle.
- Face the cork away from you and everyone else, turn the bottle, yes, the bottle, slowly until you feel the cork easing out. Don't remove the cork immediately until you hear a low hiss rather than a loud pop.

HOW TO POUR SPARKLING WINES AND CHAMPAGNE
- Hold each glass at an angle and pour against the side to preserve the bubbles.
- Pour a small amount into each glass at first and when the bubbles subside, top up to three-quarters full.
- To prevent drips, twist the bottle slightly as you right it.

Beer

Although your teens will in all probability drink straight from the can or bottle, but if they do decide to pour it into a glass, for instance at the table during supper, this is the way to do it.

- Hold the glass at an angle and pour the beer against the side to reduce the amount of 'head' – two fingers is about right.

Cheers!

Sam: 'I was shown at an early age how to open and pour a glass of wine (more for my mum than anything else), but it is always nice to sit at a table and know if I'm asked I can pour a glass of wine correctly.'

seven

Respectful Behaviour

how to behave with others

Adults – Respect

All adults, regardless of position, sex, colour or race should be treated with the same respect by us all, child, teenager or adult. But children and teenagers can sometimes behave differently to those they perceive as not having much authority and will, for example, happily take their school lunch without looking up and saying, 'Hello' or 'Thank you' to the dinner lady.

The example we set will be copied by our children, so the way we treat waiters, cashiers and door-to-door sales-men will be copied by our children.

If you have a mother's help or au-pair in your home, insist that your teenager treats them with respect and not as some type of slave to tidy their rooms and bring them endless snacks.

A friend of mine was an air-hostess for many years and cannot get over the time she asked a teenager if he would like a drink.

'Yeah, I'll have a coke,' he said. 'Don't you think you should say please?' she asked politely. The confused teen's mother, who had overheard, replied, 'You don't have to say thank you to her, she's just a waitress.' Unbelievable.

The adults who have to deal with our teens on a daily basis and who are leaving their profession in droves because of the lack of respect they receive are teachers. I simply don't understand how children as young as five can stand up and proclaim, 'I know my rights.' But what about the teacher's right to teach a class of children who can obey simple instructions and show respect for an adult?

Please make sure that your teens treat their teachers with the utmost respect. If at any point they feel they are being mentally bullied by a teacher, they should tell you and you can both deal with it, rather than trying to deal with it by pointing out 'their rights' in the classroom.

Teenagers should also respect their elders, even if you think this sounds old-fashioned, and show it by holding doors open, standing to one side in corridors or narrow pavements to let them pass, giving up their seat on public transport and generally being courteous to them. If they see an adult they know, perhaps a friend of their parents, or a neighbour, rather than just nod a sullen acknowledgement or look the other way, they should stop and talk to them for just a few minutes.

> **Katherine:** 'I've got a part-time job at a bar/restaurant a few evenings a week to help with uni, and I cannot believe how rude people are. One woman actually clicked her fingers to attract my attention, very few say please or thank you and one girl said snootily, 'We'll have five shooters.' When I asked what type she condescendingly said, 'Well vodka, obviously.' When I pointed out that we had fifteen varieties of vodka shooters, she said 'Any,' so I asked the barman to make up five of the vodka and Tabasco shooters and to go heavy with the Tabasco.'

Simple Courtesies

We all lead such busy lives these days that simple courtesies often get by-passed, but the tiniest amount of thought would not impede our lives but would certainly make someone else's a great deal more pleasant. Take, for instance supermarkets. I'm sure most of us are guilty at some time or another of fumbling to pay at the checkout and handing the money over, saying 'Thanks, bye,' without once actually looking at the cashier. Or we may have walked through a shop door without holding it open for the person behind us.

All the following courtesies are easily taught by explanation, example and reminders and they will be all highly appreciated by the recipient.

Please and Thank You

There is simply no substitute for these words and no reason why children, teenagers or adults should not use them each and every time they are appropriate. It seems so obvious it should not even have to be written about.

Teenagers and adults who certainly should know better can still forget the all important 'Please' and 'Thank you' or sometimes they are lost as their sentences trail off. Teenagers are still our children and although we don't want to embarrass them (or ourselves) in front of anyone by asking, 'What's the magic word?' a quiet reminder to say please or thank you will be necessary.

It is also very important for them to start looking people in the eye when they say it, whether it's parents, shop assistants, teachers or waiters. For example, if a girl is in a shop looking through a rail of jeans when an assistant comes up to help, it would be very rude of her to say, 'Have you got these in a size 10,' without looking at her or even saying please. Or, for instance, it is extremely rude not to look at waiters when they serve you your meal. How many of us are guilty of just looking straight ahead or talking to other guests and either muttering a 'Thanks' or saying nothing?

Encourage and teach this at home – even if you are giving your teen his supper on his lap in front of the TV, he must turn to look at you and say, 'Thank you.'

Make sure you are always polite, whether it is to your children, trades people or shop assistants and remember to thank other car drivers if they show courtesy towards you. Apart from the obvious use of please and thank you, there are many more opportunities for teenagers to apply them during their normal school day.

For instance, getting off the school bus, turning to the driver with a smile and 'Thanks, bye' would probably be appreciated and noticed amongst the dozens who shuffle on and off and say nothing.

Your teenagers should be reminded to thank the dinner ladies at school and to always make the effort to thank a teacher who has organized something, whether it is a trip, a show or an art exhibition. Teachers put a great deal of their own time into projects at school and a thank you from a grateful pupil goes a long way to making their effort worthwhile. The appreciation felt by the teacher should cause him to focus on that pupil in the future and for such a small effort it can reap many rewards.

Thank You Letters …

In this era of mobile phones, emails and text messaging, the art of a written thank you letter seems almost Dickensian – as long as one says thank you, does it much matter how it's done?

But to the recipient of the thank you message, it does. Very little time or effort goes into a 'thnk u nan 4 the CD, lv Jack'. However, a short hand-written note or card shows effort and thought, even though the thought has probably been at a parent's insistence. And it isn't just small children that need reminding to write these letters.

Tell them if there is anything relevant to the particular person they are writing to so they can mention it in the letter, for example, '… I hear you are moving house soon, I hope it all goes smoothly.' Also get your children to enquire how the person they are writing to is. 'How are you Nana? I hope you are fit and well. Looking forward to seeing you soon.' Prompting children to enquire about someone's well-being, whether in a letter or verbally, teaches them to take an interest in other people.

By the time children are teenagers, if they stay over at a friend's house or are taken out to supper by a friend's parents they should write a short letter of thanks.

To encourage your teenagers to write thank you notes, invest in some black or brightly coloured writing paper or cards and silver or gold pens to make the task a bit more interesting. And yes, you will have to keep on at them until they do it.

... and Everyday Letters

Although letter writing has almost become a lost art amongst the younger generation, try encouraging your teen to write the occasional one. Texts are designed for quick messages and last for just moments before being deleted, but letters can last a lifetime. Explain how receiving a chatty letter, especially hand-written, has such a 'feel-good' factor to it that it's worth making the effort to write one. Grandparents, god-parents, friends and family living away from home would be so grateful, not just for the news but to know that someone took some time out of their busy lives to do something just for them.

And if this generation stops writing letters, will this be the end of the 'billet doux'? How sad it will be for them to reach our age and not be able to look back with laughter/tears/heartache/pity to read their old love letters. So when your teenager is either walking on air in love or at their wit's end over an argument or misunderstanding, suggest they write their 'amour' a short letter.

Excuse Me

There are many uses for these two words. It should be used to attract another person's attention if they need to ask something, for example, 'Excuse me please, do you know where the train station is?' It is also used to interrupt a conversation, as in, 'Excuse me for interrupting, but if we don't leave now we will miss our bus.'

Excuse me is also used as an apology. For instance, we should all learn to say excuse me if we need to pass close by someone in a congested space such as on public transport or in a supermarket as a way of saying, 'Sorry, but I'm going to have to squeeze by you.' Children and teenagers should also learn to use it by way of apology if they sneeze, cough or pass wind (noisily!) in close proximity to another person.

Coughing and Sneezing

Some manners they were taught as children sometimes get lost or mislaid in the transition to teenagers, and they may well need a reminder. Everyone should always cover their mouth if they are coughing and cover their mouth and nose if they are sneezing, preferably into a tissue. They should do this whether they are alone or in company, in an enclosed space or outside, and then say, 'Excuse me.'

Nobody wants to sit at a table eating, or stand in a queue, or even walk along the pavement only to have someone, child or adult, sneeze or cough all over them. It's unhygienic and extremely unpleasant.

Explain that if they are sitting at a table eating, they must turn their heads away from the table and the person next to them if they feel a cough or sneeze coming. However, if they have diners on each side they will have to try and push back their chair to cough and sneeze (out of the line of fire) then say, 'Excuse me.'

Belching and Burping

Teenagers seem to take great satisfaction from thinking they appear adult by belching loudly at the table. They mainly do it because they realize they can and it also usually gets a big laugh from a younger sibling or, sadly, sometimes from a parent. If your teen is belching at the table it is usually for attention, so rather than laugh or make a huge fuss about how rude they are being, simply say, 'Please don't do that at the table,' and ignore them, and make sure you give them the right type of attention by talking to them. Away from the table tell younger children to ignore their older sibling when he belches.

If the belching continues with excuses such as it's the beer or coke, simply ban them drinking anything fizzy within an hour of and during eating. That usually stops it, either because it was a genuine excuse or because they actually want their beer or fizzy drink.

'Pardon' not 'Wot'

This is very self-explanatory: try and get your teenagers to say 'Pardon?' not 'What?' or 'Wot?' as it just sounds so much more polite. Although when your children become adolescents, even if they have grasped the use of the word pardon, they seem to use 'Wot?' as often as possible. As in, 'We're having your favourite, roast chicken, for supper tonight,' 'Wot?' 'Have a good day at school, I'll see you tonight,' 'Wot?' Simply ask them not to say, 'Wot?' but 'Pardon?' if they genuinely did not hear, or point out that what you said was a statement not a question.

Shaking Hands

WHY DO WE SHAKE HANDS?

Shaking hands originated from the right arm being held out to show that you were unarmed. Nowadays, psychological research indicates that even the briefest physical contact with another in an obviously non-aggressive manner will improve strangers' dispositions towards each other and enforce the belief that they will both be honest and helpful. So now you know.

Shaking hands is also an accepted form of apology and teenagers from about the age of fifteen can use it at school if, for instance, they've annoyed a particular teacher. They could go to the teacher privately and apologize for their behaviour and offer to shake hands. Hopefully, the apology will be accepted by the teacher, who will no doubt be impressed by such mature behaviour.

WHEN TO USE IT

Shaking hands is used as a normal greeting between adult friends. Teach your teens to use it when they are introduced to an adult. And even from the age of sixteen male teenagers meeting male teenagers for the first time often shake hands.

HOW TO SHAKE HANDS

If you haven't before, now is the time to explain to your teenagers that 'you never get a second chance to make a first impression', as the saying goes. Rightly or wrongly, many of us judge a person's character by their handshake. To me and to many other people the limp handshake and the averted eyes scream that this person is wet, lacking in personality and ineffectual. But eye-to-eye contact and a firm handshake say open, honest, confident and capable. This is not to say we are correct but it is our first impression and it could eventually mean the difference between getting the job or not. Even women should give a firm handshake, and not just offer a few limp fingers.

Teach your daughters and sons the following:

- They should extend their right hand.
- They should then look the person in the eye.
- They should always smile.
- It is essential to place their hand fully in the palm of the other hand and give a firm handshake, the emphasis being on firm, not bone-crushing or limp.
- They should introduce themselves if it is the first time.
- Only two or three shakes are necessary and they should not be too fast.
- If they think their hands are a bit clammy they should try and dry them first without being noticed. However, if they shake hands with someone who has clammy hands they should try to avoid immediately wiping their hands down their trousers or skirt, although this is everyone's instant reaction.

Sam: 'After playing many games of hockey, I've seen many good players on the other team, well-built, skilled, good-looking, the sort of guy you'd generally respect. But then after the game, if his handshake is weak and pathetic, I'd think what a loser.'

Kissing Each Cheek

The other way of greeting friends is kissing on both cheeks. Even though women have been doing this for years (sometimes only air kissing accompanied by a 'Mwah, mwah, let's do lunch,') there's absolutely no reason why your teenagers can't greet their friends and in some instances your friends, in exactly the same way. The only prompt you can give is that these pecks on the cheek are more a brushing of the cheeks; no one wants a slobbery, wet kiss on the cheek!

Taking Coats

Sons and daughters should, without having to be asked, help lady guests and even men guests with their coats. If they have never been taught, teach them how to hold the coat open so the wearer can slip their hands in easily and then ease the coat onto their shoulders. It's amazing the amount of men who think helping with coats is throwing you a crumpled mess and letting you sort it out for yourself.

The flattering attention your son will receive from grateful (and surprised) ladies and girlfriends will not go unnoticed.

Opening Doors and Ladies First

Your own opinions on feminism may determine whether you think boys should still be brought up to show women traditional courtesies but in my opinion many women now and I'm sure in the future will still very much appreciate them. Not to teach them is putting them at a disadvantage, as their girlfriends or possible future female boss just might be women who do appreciate such courtesies.

Hopefully, you've taught your children from a young age, but even if you haven't it's never too late. Teach sons and daughters to be aware and hold doors open for adults, whether it's a shop door, your own front door or a car door. Also teach your daughter to be gracious if someone opens the door for her. I've heard guys complain that girls have said, 'I can do it myself,' when they have tried to open doors for them. A smile and 'Thank you very much,' is all that is needed and would be far more appreciated.

However, if it is a revolving door, then apparently the man should go first to keep the door moving, and if it's a lift, whoever gets to the open lift doors first should hold them open for everyone else.

Also explain to your son that if he and a member of the opposite sex both go to do something at the same time, for instance, walk through a door or approach a salesperson, he should allow the female to go first.

Answering the Telephone

Answering the telephone?! You're probably thinking, 'A teen who can't answer the phone? But they're never off it.' And you're absolutely right, but have you ever rung a home line which is answered by a teenager? Funnily enough, 'Yeah?' doesn't do it for me.

Long gone are the days of answering in a terribly prim voice, 'Wimbledon two four two four', and nowadays

because of security we no longer need to answer the phone by mentioning our telephone number. So it's not that difficult to say, 'Hello,' and if the caller asks to speak to someone but doesn't say their name, 'Who's speaking please?' would be appropriate if not ground breaking. And in the unlikely event that the phone call is not actually for your teen but they know the caller, they should respond by saying, 'How are you?' or 'Mum said you've been on holiday, did you have a good time?' We know teenagers can talk on the phone, we have phone bills to prove it, so the least they can do is to make a minor effort to talk to your friends when they call (and have the good fortune to get through).

And it's worth making sure there is always a pen and paper near the phone, as with the best will in the world there is very little chance of your teenagers remembering any messages.

Reliability

If you say you are going to do something, you do it. Our teenagers will learn this lesson by your approach to reliability as much as anything, so if you say you will do something for them by a certain time, you do it.

They must realize how important it is that they can be counted on, relied on to do what they have said they will do (I'm sure we all know a few adults who we wish would learn). Around the home you should be able to make requests such as, 'I've got to go out, but please put the roast in the oven at 6pm. You will do it, won't you?' If they forget, the consequence is no roast for supper. And however simple the request, if they do it, thank and praise them.

Even if they have let you down on a couple of occasions avoid labelling them as unreliable, for example by saying, 'You're the same with everything, you cannot be relied on to do anything.'

Tell them that often enough and they'll soon live up to this reputation.

Teenagers can often resent having to give up their free time for a prior engagement, perhaps a hockey match or a drama rehearsal. Suddenly on the morning they don't want to be in the 'stupid' team or play. Explain that is their choice, but they cannot let people down at the last minute who are depending upon them to be there, so they must go today and after the match or rehearsal explain why they no longer wish to continue.

Teenagers who are not taught how to be reliable will grow up and constantly let friends and co-workers down. Even their friends will soon get fed up with them if they continually say they will go with them somewhere and then at the last minute decide not to. Of course, everyone has a right to a change of mind, but all involved parties must be given advanced notice of the change of arrangements.

But the more reliable you are as a parent, the more natural it will be for your children to become reliable, so think very carefully before promising to do something for them that you can't actually carry out.

Point out to your teenagers the importance of being on time (although we know what lousy time-keepers they are), whether it is for lessons, social dates or appointments. Explain how discourteous it is to be late but if they are, always to make sure they apologize.

Katherine: 'My mum asked me to put clean sheets on the guest bed whilst she was shopping. I had every intention of doing it, it's just that it wasn't my number one priority and mum came home before I had got round to doing it. I'll never forget when she saw the bed still unmade, she came to see me and when she's angry with us, which is not often to be honest, she never shouts but drops her voice really low, which is fairly scary, and said very firmly, "Katherine, how dare you let me down, I relied on you to do that. Please don't ever let anyone down again." And to be honest, I haven't.'

Apologies

It goes without saying that there will be times when your teenagers will have to apologize for something they have said or done. The way in which, 'I'm sorry,' or 'I apologize,' is said is vitally important to the recipient. A spitting out of the words whilst looking at the ground is a non-starter; it's clearly stating, 'Actually, I'm not sorry and therefore my apology is meaningless.'

'Sorry' is a hard word to convey, as it takes humility whilst giving the ego and pride a kick in the teeth. And there will be plenty of times during adolescence that your teenagers will probably have to use it, for instance footballs going into gardens, broken promises, poor behaviour or being late, to name just a few, so it is best they get the finest example and that is from you. During your teen's adolescence there will be times when you need to apologize, perhaps for losing your temper and shouting at them, or for being particularly disagreeable (yes, we can be like that too).

If the thought of having to say a face-to-face apology is just too much for them, suggest they write a short note. Perhaps if it's a neighbour they have upset, to keep all relationships on an even keel, suggest they go round to apologize with a small bunch of flowers (which you have funded).

I recently had a conversation with my daughter Katherine about the urgency of her finishing the cartoons for this book:

'Katherine, it's getting beyond a joke, I have to hand the draft in this week.'

'It's cool, mum, I'll get them done.'

'But you've been telling me that for the past three months.'

'It's okay. It's cool, I will.'

'Actually it's not cool Katherine, I have a contract and seeing as you're getting paid for this, you also have a responsibility.'

'Okay, chill out.'

'Actually, it's not okay, I need these cartoons, which I have been asking for, for months, and although you say you're going to do them, I have nothing!'

'It's okay.'

At this point I lost it completely and shrieked, 'Actually, it's not f***ing okay.'

With that I slammed the phone down and promptly burst into tears. I felt so ashamed that I had to get my husband to ring and apologize on my behalf and I rang the next day and apologized myself and so did Katherlne.

respect in the home

Teenagers are members of the family and while they live with their parents at home they should contribute to the housework. As anyone with teenagers will know, they would be quite happy to exist in a darkened room amidst a mountain of empty cans, half-filled mouldy coffee mugs, screwed-up tissues, sweet wrappers and empty crisp bags littering the floor.

One perennial moan from parents is that their teenage children are so lazy and do nothing around the house to help. If they have been helping and doing chores from a young age, they will usually help when asked; it's just that as teenagers they are often in their room and out of sight. However, if parents have seldom, if ever enlisted their children's help, and they suddenly ask them to vacuum the sitting room, they will be greeted with a confused look accompanied by the perennial 'Wot?' Some teenagers, when asked to do something, will say in a very agreeable voice, 'Yeah, sure,' and you'll think that was easy, but they'll never actually get round to doing it. They genuinely thought when they agreed that they would, but never managed to get away from the TV to carry it out and then found something more important to do, like ringing their friends, and totally forgot about it.

So to be successful when you ask a teenager to help and to cause as little stress as possible to all concerned, try and follow a few simple rules (when possible). The most important point to remember is when you ask a teenager to do anything you must state that it must be carried out straightaway. If you say, 'Can you vacuum the sitting room today, please darling,' you may as well say, 'It's all right I'll vacuum the sitting room myself,' because they will never get around to it. And don't ask them when they are in the middle of their favourite soap or TV programme, because their reply will be, 'Yes, sure, when this has finished,' which means never.

Cajoling rather than ordering is absolutely vital, as in 'Darling, here's the vacuum, please just vacuum this room and tidy up in here whilst you're watching this programme. It would really help me, and can you do it right now please. Thanks, gorgeous.' But the ordering approach, as in, 'This place is like a pig-sty now get off your lazy bum, tidy up and vacuum it. NOW,' will just make them resentful and open to replies, such as, 'Well, I didn't make all the bloody mess, those are your shoes over there, so why don't you do it?'

And when they have done the job, praise and thank them, 'Fantastic job, thank you so much darling, it looks great,' and in your most cajoling tone you will have to add, 'Now could you just pop the vacuum cleaner under the stairs, thank you so much,' otherwise they will leave it in the middle of the room (for years if they're not asked to put it away).

But what if the cajoling approach doesn't work, and when you go back into the sitting room, it is still in a mess and they are just sitting there watching TV? Turn the TV off, amid the cries of, 'Wot you doing?' Stay calm, don't shout, but say in a level voice, 'I asked for your help in cleaning up this room and I expect it, please don't let me down,' (and in softer tones try and get them to empathize) 'Darling, I could really do with your help and I would really appreciate it, so please do it now.' Show some physical affection, like stroking their cheek or putting your hand over theirs. Give them the responsibility and make them feel as though they are helping you out rather than being ordered to help just because they are children. Teenagers hate being ordered to do anything and it is an open invitation for complete defiance and resentment.

If they still refuse to help, simply and calmly point out that if you have to do the job yourself you will not have time to drive them to their friend's house. Ask them if they understand what you are saying and repeat it, no job done, no lift. And if this doesn't get them to do it, when the time comes and they want that lift, quietly remind them of what you had said. Explain that the offer of a lift was in their hands, all they had to do was what they were asked, but they chose not to do it, thus foregoing their lift. Stick to your guns, do not give in, regardless of whines and moans, and don't be tempted by apologies and promises to do the job tomorrow. Tonight they will have to forego going to their friends (unless they do it right away).

However, because life isn't easy, if you know that this particular evening was a special party, date, concert or dance they had been looking forward to and you can see that they are not getting on with the chore, rather than cause world war three by refusing to take them, a couple of hours before the time they should leave, you need to take some action. Ask them to turn the TV or music off, explain that you know how important tonight is to them but you will stick to your word if the job isn't done, then cajole them into starting. It is important that they do the job, otherwise two things will happen, both of which will make you feel awful. One, your teen will cry, beg and plead for you to drop them off, and if you give in they have got what they wanted without doing as asked and you will feel resentful and angry with yourself for giving in. Two, if you refuse and hold out, their begging and pleading will quickly turn to spiteful name calling and you will end up feeling guilty and upset all night, so no one benefits. All you want is to show your teen that if a deal is made it must be kept, even if this means you partly help them to get the chore done. That's when you both benefit, the chore has been done, the teen has gone for the big night out and you can relax (with a large drink by now) knowing you haven't given in. (Phew! Who ever wanted to be a parent?)

The easiest chores in which to enrol teenagers' help are those that can be done in front of the TV, like dusting, polishing and vacuuming, folding the contents of the washing basket, pairing up clean socks and ironing. They are more likely to help with jobs in the kitchen if you are in there with them, so perhaps whilst you are preparing supper, they could empty or fill the dishwasher, wash or dry dishes, lay the table or help chop up veg or make a salad.

Always remember to thank them and say what a great help they were to you. Just occasionally, if they have been helping without moaning and have done a good job, surprise them with a treat such as a magazine or pay for them to go the cinema with a friend, but don't get into the habit of bribing them to do something.

Tidying their bedroom is, of course, an entirely different issue (page 233).

> **Sam:** 'I have no problems when asked to vacuum a room as long as I don't have to go and get it or put it away and if possible in a room where I can watch MTV and *The OC*.'

how to behave in public

Much is written in the media about the behaviour of teenagers in public, the way they throw their rubbish down in the streets, take up the whole of the pavement in groups, swear loudly and are basically totally inconsiderate to other members of the public. It can be very intimidating and perhaps twenty years ago many adults would have been bold enough to tell them about their poor behaviour, but they definitely won't now in case they receive a torrent of verbal abuse or, worse, physical abuse.

By registering your disapproval or approval of different situations, your teenagers will know what is acceptable and what is not. Obviously, parents who always leave their litter on the seat when they exit a train carriage simply teach their children that this sort of behaviour is acceptable. Hopefully, you didn't. Remember, children and teens will learn just as much from the way they see you behave as from what you say.

On Public Transport

Even though you may have taught them how to behave with you, once they start travelling alone or with their friends, it's worth reminding them that there will be other members of the public with them and to remember:

- Wait until everyone is off before they try and get on.
- Be courteous to ticket collectors and other travellers.
- Do not push past people and if they accidentally knock into someone, apologize.

- No feet on the seats.
- Keep voices down.
- Keep personal CD players and iPods low, even with ear-phones.
- Turn mobiles and game boys to mute when playing games.
- Bin their litter.
- No swearing if they can be overheard.
- Give a hand if they see someone struggling to get a pushchair or suitcase onto the train or bus.
- If there is a group of them with just a few other people in a carriage and they suspect they have made too much noise, simply say, 'Sorry about the noise,' as they leave.
- Keep mobile calls to a minimum (see Mobile Phones, page 229).
- Make outgoing calls in uncrowded passageways or between carriages.
- Never, ever try out all the ring tones where they can be overheard.
- Don't eat hot or fried food as the smell for other travellers is disgusting.
- Take off back packs and carry them in front of them.
- Boys can give up their seat to a woman of any age or an elderly man.
- Girls should give up their seat to pregnant women and the elderly. Your reaction at reading this will probably be 'GET REAL', but if you have already taught your child how to behave on public transport, you will also probably know their weakness, like having their personal stereo too loud or too many phone calls; so you only have to mention what is relevant. And say it in a very casual,

'Bye, have a good time, and oh, by the way, don't forget to keep the stereo down,' or, 'I know I don't have to tell you but no feet on the seats ... enjoy yourself.'

Don't panic! Even if you have never taught them how to behave on public transport, simply start with, 'Now you're responsible enough to travel on your own ...' and go on to give them a couple of the above suggestions about what to do. Then, when you travel with them point out or demonstrate some others.

Remember, rather than tell them directly what not to do, which may be met with a vacant stare, introduce it into conversation, for example, 'I was on the train and this teenager's iPod was so loud I could have sung along to the tune. Thank goodness I know you'd never be that selfish.'

Sam: 'Occasionally, if the carriage is empty and I'm feeling absolutely knackered I sometimes put my feet up on the opposite seats, but if someone came in and gave me a disapproving look, I would take them off.'

In Public Places

Your teenagers will be out in public with their friends far more than they will be with you, so you can only hope that they're not terrorizing the general public. You can't be responsible for what other teenagers or their friends do, but if you can be reasonably sure that your child won't be behaving badly you can relax. In most cases, teenagers don't intentionally mean to intimidate the public; they are just not conscious of how they are behaving and are not aware of other people. The crux of the matter is that manners are about showing courtesy to other people, but during adolescence teenagers are consumed with themselves and give little or no thought to anyone outside their group of friends. But we can't let them off that easily.

Either by bringing the issues up in conversation, by good example or by simply reminding them, they need to have a grasp of the following ways to behave in public:

- No swearing where they can be overheard.
- If they are walking on pavements or paths with friends, move to single file to let oncomers pass on the outside.
- Assist parents with pushchairs and generally be aware of other people.
- Resist eating in the streets. Surely they can take five minutes to sit somewhere.
- Bin their rubbish.
- Respect public property.
- Be aware of other people, open doors, help with pushchairs, and don't push and shove.
- Now don't laugh, but even help elderly people across the road. If they just take their arm and escort them across it would mean so much to someone and yet take less than a minute (unless they walk very slowly) to help.
- No skateboarding on pavements, airports, shops or anywhere where it is likely to be a nuisance.

SPITTING

It's disgusting (even on a football pitch) but even more so in public, and it is totally unnecessary. Explain that this is a really repellent habit and beg them never to do it.

Sam: 'Spitting is disgusting, I try not to be anal but when I see my friends do it I do tell them not to and explain to them how ridiculous they look.'

CHEWING GUM

Everybody these days seems to chew gum which is fine, as long as it is chewed with mouths closed, and disposed of before a conversation with someone. It's the disposing of it that has become a problem, and yet it is so simple to put the used gum either in its original wrapper or in a piece of tissue or paper and put it in the bin. Now is that so hard?

In Cinemas and Theatres

Now there are a few hard and fast rules here and teenagers need to be reminded of them because a group of noisy, selfish adolescents can really ruin the enjoyment for so many people. This is one area, along with museums and exhibitions, where you should actually explain to your teens the dos and don'ts.

Naturally, they must turn off their mobile phone and not resort to playing games or texting, however awful the movie is – if it's that bad, leave. If they have to shuffle past people already seated they should say, 'Excuse me' and 'Thank you', and, if the programme has already started, apologize. They should get to their seats and sit down with the minimum of fuss, no changing who sits next to who, basically sit down and shut-up. No talking during the film and if they have to make a comment to their friend to quickly whisper, not to engage in conversation. Ask them not to put their feet up on the seats in front and to be careful not to kick them either.

FOOD AND THE CINEMA

Hot cheesy nachos, hot dogs, burgers and chips should be eaten and finished before entering the auditorium; no one wants to sit in what smells like a deep fat-fryer. And as for sweet wrappers, why oh why does someone have to fiddle with a sweet wrapper for the entire length of a film – have they no conception of how irritating it is for anyone within ten rows?

If you occasionally go to the cinema to see a film with your teens, you'll have a good idea of how they behave.

A TV producer told me that she sat a few seats away but in the same row as a teenager who played with a sweet paper for the entire film, despite her glares and 'Sshhs' at him. At the end of the movie when the lights came on, she said to the boy in a very 'I am so p****d off with you' voice how the noise of the wrapper had completely ruined the film for her and did he realize how totally selfish he had been? The boy, she said, looked visibly shocked, but the rest of the audience started calling, 'Hear, Hear,' (or equivalent) and broke into applause. The teenager was clearly unaware of his behaviour, so as parents let's make sure our teens are aware. Now they are going to adult movies we don't want them to let themselves down by not acting like one.

   As an adult, if you are ever in a cinema and someone is constantly talking or being irritating, if they don't stop when they are asked, go and get the manager to throw them out.

> **Sam:** 'My friends and I also get really annoyed when a group of people of our age think it's cool to be loud and obnoxious when the film is on.'

Museums and Exhibitions

Quite simply, keep voices down and don't run or climb on anything. Be aware, for example, if someone is admiring an exhibit, not to walk between the admirer and the artwork. And definitely turn off their mobiles and turn down their iPods or personal CD players! Food and drink are not usually allowed into museums but if they do sneak something in they should make sure they bin the rubbish on their way out and not leave it perched on an exhibit.

total respect — how not to embarrass your children

First, you may think why not? But let's not dwell on that, just believe me, you'll get more respect if you don't.

Although many teenagers want to be individual in their style and appear 'cool' to their peers, when it comes to their parents they want normal.

Here's a quick list of no-nos:

- Dress your age, no one wants a mum or dad dressed like a teenager.
- Don't try and talk the 'hip' talk.

'Dad, please no, not the air guitar. You're so gay!'

- Don't try and embrace and kiss your teenagers in front of their friends.
- Don't show photos of them to friends or discuss some silly episode that happened when they were three.
- Don't swear in front of them.
- Don't drink too much (especially if you become all gooey and cuddly towards them).
- Don't kiss and embrace your partner in front of them.
- Don't make double entendres or jokes about sex.
- Don't try and be 'cool' in front of their friends.
- Don't dance, especially with an air guitar.

You have been warned.

teenage affairs

eight

Relationships

the dating game

First loves, unrequited love, jealousy, broken hearts, fluttery stomachs: we've all been there and now your little darlings are about to experience the full gamut of emotions. The thought that some spotty oick is going to be pawing

'Mum, they're kissing!'

your beautiful little girl (already!) may send shivers down your spine, but that spotty oick was also someone's beautiful little baby boy (and his parents think he still is).

The age at which teenagers become attracted to the opposite sex appears to get younger and younger. When I was thirteen I was still going to marry my pony and seeing what happened to my first marriage, I sometimes wish I had! The age at which your children become interested has a lot to do with puberty, their peers, programmes they watch and magazines they read.

Once they start going out just with their friends or with particular boy/girl friends, ask for a list of their friends' mobile and home phone numbers in case of an emergency, but don't go and abuse this information by ringing around every friend if your teen is ten minutes late. At whatever age you start to let them go out with a mixed crowd or on a one-to-one basis, boundaries must still be in place, namely what time they are home. But again, the way you tell them what time to be home should be open to agreement between the two of you, which will make it far more likely that it will be adhered to. Take into consideration where they are going and what time buses or public transport run. There's no point saying 11pm if you know the bus doesn't arrive near your house until 11.10pm.

In the event that they are held up, they must, MUST ring and let you know why, where they are, who they are with or whether they are alone, and at what time they will be home. Explain that three lates in a month will automatically mean forfeiting a weekend. Tell them what the consequences for their actions will be, so there is no confrontation afterwards. And just like when they were little, if you threaten a punishment it must be carried out if they cross the boundaries. You can also explain that if after a month they have been home every time, on time, you may let them stay out one night a little later. Explain that being considerate and responsible works both ways.

But, as a parent, there will be the occasional time when you will have to get out of bed and go and pick them up because arrangements have gone awry. On these occasions don't spend the entire trip home berating them, they must know how you feel and, in all probability, they would have preferred a different outcome too.

If you consider your thirteen-year-old daughter too young to start dating, rather than saying 'No', which means she will go anyway, you should suggest she goes with a mixed group of friends for the first few dates so there are no awkward moments. Ask if the boy can come and meet her at the house so you have a chance to get to know him.

When your teenagers are fifteen or sixteen, allow them a TV in their room. If you only want to allow your teens out one night over the weekend but they want to go out both nights, suggest they invite their boy/girlfriend to the house to watch a video. Explain that if they watch TV in their bedroom there will be no locked doors and under no circumstances would you enter without knocking, asking to come in and waiting for an answer. If you have always shown respect and knocked and waited for a reply outside your children's bedroom door, and you assure them that you will not enter without notice, there is absolutely no reason for them to lock the door unless they are doing something you would not approve of. If you have boys, I believe that you have a certain obligation to your son's girl-friend's parents that you will not allow them to be in com-promising situations.

There are many areas in a teenager's life where interfer-ence from a parent is like a red rag to a bull, and talking about relationships is clearly one of them. This is a definite thin ice topic, so proceed with caution or blunder in at your peril. If you want to keep lines of communication open, stay open minded. Never tease them about the opposite sex, or say demeaning things, such as, 'Oooh, is he your boyfriend?' or 'You two seem all lovey dovey.' This is the quickest way to get your children to clam up, so try a different approach: treat them as adults.

Treat them with respect, ask normal questions and try and not sound like the Spanish Inquisition. If your daugh-ter or son is happy to talk about their friend, ask if they would like to have them over to your house. The mention of a meal may be too much to handle at first, but certainly say they are welcome for a drink, coffee or beer depending on their age. The plus of having your son or daughter with their friend or friends at home is that you know where they are and probably what they're doing!

unsuitable boy/girlfriends

When your children were little, if they had friends that you were not so keen on, you could invite different friends to play to encourage new relationships. It's quite a different kettle of fish once they are adolescents.

You will have absolutely no say over who your teenagers choose to go out with. In fact, the more you disapprove, the more likely they are to continue the relationship. It's just a way of saying, I am growing up and I am making my own decisions. So, if you are not keen on your teenager's boyfriend or girlfriend, rather than saying you think they are unsuitable, find something positive to say about them, like what lovely eyes, what a great smile, or what a good sense of humour. If your teen realizes you're not about to disapprove, they have nothing to rebel against and the relationship may well fizzle out sooner rather than later. Another good ploy is to invite them around for supper, the benefit being that you may actually get to know and like the person or they will feel so out-of-their-league that they will break the relationship off.

Not all their friends will meet your approval

I once read about a woman who said she went out with someone much longer than she would have done just because her parents disapproved.

However, if you feel your teen is being led astray into petty crime, alcohol or drug abuse, you must intervene. Ask them to sit down with you and voice your concerns, starting by saying that you like the 'friend' but are concerned about whatever the problem is. Ask if they know why their friend behaves in that manner; perhaps he is unhappy at home or perhaps he has a more deep-rooted problem which, as a friend, your child should try to help with. Point out that going down the same route as their friend is not helping anyone. Give them plenty of opportunity to talk if they want to, and if they don't, at least you have spoken to them in a caring, sympathetic voice and they can mull it over.

Whatever the problem and however unsuitable you may think their boyfriend or girlfriend is, the last thing you want to do is to start laying down the law and refusing permission to see them again as this is likely to have the opposite effect. Shouting, 'I forbid you to see him again,' or similar will work against you. If you are really upset and worried about their boy/girlfriend, ask a good friend or relative that your child respects to have a quiet word.

Fran: 'My step-mum and dad weren't the biggest fans of one of my ex-boyfriends. Although I knew this, they never made it awkward by saying stupid comments in front of him and were always polite. They accepted the fact that I liked him and that it was my choice who I went out with.'

manners in relationships

Although teenagers need to find out for themselves the ups and downs of relationships, there is a rough code of ethics which may be worth discussing over dinner. Seeing that many celebrities and sports stars offer scant examples of how to behave with decency in relationships, it would not be surprising if our children thought it okay to do the same.

If you have brought your son up to open doors for girls and help them with their coats he will in all probability automatically do it. But once he starts going out with girls you can mention (or even better, get their father to mention) that it is polite to always walk on the outside of the pavement, with his girlfriend on the inside. He should also, whenever possible, see his girlfriend to her door, or onto a bus or into a taxi. If the girl has a long trip home your son could ask her to text him to say she has arrived safely. It makes girls feel protected and safe to know that someone cares about their safety. It'll also go down a storm with the girlfriend's parents.

One subject to bring up is the no-no of snogging in public. Perhaps discuss a film where the main stars have kissed in public, and say that it may be all right for the movies but watching other people suck each other's faces is seriously naff.

paying compliments

One of women's biggest complaints against men is the lack of compliments they shower on us.

Now you may think that we shouldn't have to teach boys how to pay a compliment and that it should come naturally, but it just doesn't seem to. Girls never seem to have the same problem and they are usually very open with compliments. Fortunately, teaching boys how to pay a compliment also teaches them to be observant, which will be an invaluable lesson for all areas of their life.

We all enjoy feeling flattered when we are paid a compliment whether by a fourteen-year-old boy or a seventy-year-old man. Again, the reaction boys receive from the opposite sex after they have paid a compliment should encourage them to continue.

So it's worth mentioning to your teenage boys that girlfriends love to be complimented, especially as they have probably tried on ten different outfits and spent three hours in their room getting ready. 'I like your hair that way,' or, 'You look lovely,' goes down a storm.

In fact, mention to your girls that when they are paid a compliment they should accept it graciously by simply saying, 'Thank you.' Many girls feel embarrassed when they are complimented and either deny it or get all embarrassed. If a guy says to his girlfriend, 'You look great tonight,' and she replies, all embarrassed, 'No I don't, stupid, I just look like I normally do,' he is unlikely to bother with compliments again. Of course, you can equally tell your girls to pay compliments to their boyfriends, although it comes so much more naturally to them.

You could also point out with a wry smile that mothers, grandmothers and even female teachers all occasionally like to be flattered in the form of a compliment.

Imagine the scenario: Billy is late handing in his homework, and the teacher thinks to herself, 'But didn't he say last month that he liked my new haircut?' She may well say, 'Now you really must make more effort to get it in on time in future, or I will have to take action.'

Let's try that scenario again: Billy is late handing in his homework, and the teacher thinks to herself, 'He is always so rude and disruptive in my class, I'll teach him.' She may quite possibly say, 'You can stay in this lunch-hour and do it and take a detention for Saturday morning, to make sure next week's homework won't be late.'

Sam: 'When I go out I have no problems telling a girl if they look nice. It is always appreciated and gets me that one step closer to getting with them. Some girls reply, 'Oh stop it, I just threw this on,' when it's quite obvious they were in front of the mirror for hours. Sometimes I get the 'Thank you, you're such a gentleman Sam,' which is absolute cash-back.*

---

* See Glossary, page 255.

guess who's coming to dinner?

If your teen has a regular boy/girl friend, suggest bringing them over for supper. Most teenagers will blush at the thought of this, but the day will come when they actually agree. They will only ever agree if they know for certain that you will say nothing to embarrass or humiliate them or their partner and that you will act like normal people. No 'trendy' clothes or teen speak. To show that you will be making an effort, ask your teen what interests their friend has, not because you are going to barrage them with questions, just so that you can have a general idea of what subjects to discuss. Depending on their age, find out first if your teen would like you to offer them both wine, beer or stick to soft drinks. Ask if their friend has any food preferences, as the last thing you want to happen is to cook a roast chicken if they're vegetarians.

Choose something easy and straightforward to eat, for instance if you have pasta don't choose one of the long thin varieties such as spaghetti as it's not the easiest thing to eat.

If younger children are going to be joining you, it's best to have a quiet word with them explaining there will be no rude or silly comments or saying anything to embarrass their older sibling.

breaking up

I know this is the age of technology but please try and convince your sons and daughters not to break off a relationship by text. Give the poor person who is about to get the elbow the respect of a face-to-face dismissal, or at worst a phone call or even a letter. Try and get your children to empathize with their friend's feelings and how they would feel if they were told it was 'over' by text.

Although you could say that cheating on a partner is all part of learning about relationships, it is very painful for children to be on the receiving end. They feel upset by the disloyalty of their partner and their self-esteem gets a kick in the teeth. Apart from sympathy, explain that the person who cheats suffers from insecurity and if they cheat on someone and get away with it, they will always do it. Explain that the best thing to do would be to finish with them, as they deserve so much better. After all, if they continue to see this person it could be seen as condoning such behaviour, which makes it far more likely that it will happen again.

The following advice may go against human nature, but at some appropriate time, ask them not to make derogatory comments to all their friends about their ex. It's over for whatever reason, but it is so much better to keep a dignified silence unless it's just to their best friend (who is sworn to secrecy) or family (when you can empathize or sympathize). So, basically, don't kiss and tell, just kiss and stay silent. Just think of how dignified Jackie Onassis remained, never uttering a word about her late husband, compared with some of our more recent celebs who feel the need to let the world know about their exes' every fault.

At exam time, if your teen tells you they are going to break-up with their present girl/boyfriend, ask them to wait until exams are over, as the heart-breaking news will undoubtedly cause great upset to their ex and could definitely affect academic performance. Suggest they say that they are so busy revising (we wish) that they will not be able to see so much of their friend until the exams are over, when they can drop the bombshell.

broken hearts

Comfort, cuddles, kind words and time are the only healers for a broken heart. Of course, at the time they feel that it's the end of the world, so trying to convince them that there are 'plenty more fish in the sea' or that 'he wasn't good enough for you anyway' will only fall on deaf ears. Far better to hold and comfort them and treat them to an evening in a nice restaurant or a new CD. Also, make sure that their friends are around for them to talk to.

'But, mummy, I love him!'

However, if they are broken hearted because they have found out that their partner has been two-timing them, suggest that they break off the relationship, because they deserve more respect.

sex

Underneath teenagers' adult bravado, they are in fact very insecure and vulnerable.

Unfortunately, whether it's TV, films, magazines or newspapers, this generation is being constantly exposed to a celebrity culture which incorrectly promotes the idea that having loads of sexual partners is cool and you must be popular if everyone sleeps with you. So sadly, many youngsters, who we know at this age are desperate for approval, will have sex to prove that not only are they obviously attractive but also popular. Only support from parents and good friends will help to build up their self-respect and convince them that they are genuinely attractive and popular without having to resort to casual sex.

Peer pressure is one of the strongest factors in teenage sex, followed by pressure from boyfriends and curiosity. Adolescence involves a powerful mix of biological factors and a desire to conform to what they think is the norm.

They will receive sex education at school but they need to be told a few more social facts by their parents. Research has actually shown that adolescents are most likely to adopt their parents' attitudes to teenage sex if parents are willing and comfortable to discuss it and related topics. And don't worry – talking about sex does not increase your children's sexual activity, but it's imperative they know your feelings on the subject and that you talk to them about the importance of contraception.

It is highly unlikely in these times that teenagers are going to wait until they're in their twenties to start sexual relations, but there are a few facts they should know. They won't wish to listen, but explain that if they think they are old enough to have sex, they are certainly old enough to listen. Be brief, don't lecture, make sure you cannot be overheard and don't be surprised if your adolescents are excruciatingly embarrassed when you broach the subject.

Point out to your teenagers that they should at least wait until they have met someone they really like and are in a proper relationship. Explain that sex should only be part of a long-term relationship and not used as some sort of emotional currency in short-term dalliances, however much they fancy their partner. There's no harm in mentioning that sex is far more than just a physical act and, in all reality, can be pretty miserable without the bond of a strong emotional relationship, but they'd never find a friend to admit it.

Explain to your sons that having sex with a girl under sixteen, however well they know each other, is illegal and can be treated as statutory rape. Also, if they do not use contraception and the girl becomes pregnant, they will be responsible for paying for that child until it reaches sixteen. Also, as a father they will have to face the responsibilities of being a father even if they don't live with the mother.

Some things never change and regardless of the leaps we've made in equality for women, girls who sleep around are still known as 'easy' and boys who do so aren't. If you suspect your daughter is having sexual relations in each short-term relationship she enters, and she doesn't seem prepared to listen to the argument that boys would respect her a whole lot more if she didn't give in so easily and her relationships might actually last longer, the safest option is to put her on the pill. The shock of you suggesting this might make her think twice about her actions, otherwise take her to a family planning clinic or your local doctor.

Explain that a big deal is made about sex but they should not feel pressured by friends – although they may feel that the whole world is having sex most of the time, the truth is that it simply isn't true.

Finish with something along the lines of, 'You know as a responsible parent I have to say all this, but I know I don't have to worry about you because you're so responsible anyway and I trust you to do the right thing.'

The day will eventually come when your teen asks if they can have their boy/girlfriend to stay over. They mean in their bed. This is your house, and regardless of their reasons or arguments, if you are not comfortable with this idea, offer their friend a spare bed or your teen can sleep on the sofa and give up their bed to their guest. Parents of sons, I believe, have a moral obligation to the girlfriend's parents to do the right thing.

Teenagers who suspect they are gay feel very isolated. However normal it is for adult gays to 'come out', teenagers are terrified of being bullied, ostracized and teased. The way in which you talk about homosexuals over the years will influence when your children decide to tell you. Snide comments, jokes or an intolerant attitude to gays will only make your teen feel more isolated. So whether or not you suspect your child is gay, always show tolerance when talking about the subject.

nine

Major Teenage Issues

bullying

We know that bullying can have devastating effects on children, but recent American research has reported that it can have long-term effects, especially when started in adolescence. Adults who were bullied as teens can suffer low self-esteem and suffer higher levels of depression during their adult life.

During their teens, bullied children can suffer low self-esteem, depression, anxiety, fear and social isolation. Some will turn to alcohol or drugs and some will start to carry weapons. Bullies can pick on someone for all types of reasons: their race, size, intellect, the way they talk or even the colour of their hair. Bullying tends to be more common amongst younger teens than older teens and boys are more likely to be involved than girls. Boys will bully boys by name calling, physical violence and intimidating threats, and by making fun of them, whilst girls being bullied tend to be the targets of nasty or sexual rumours and comments.

Warning signs to look out for:

- Becoming withdrawn;
- Feigning illness to miss school;

- Damaged or torn clothing;
- Cuts and bruising;
- A drop in grades at school;
- Becoming upset and reluctance to talk;
- Fear of reading text messages;
- Stealing money or always running out of allowance with nothing to show for it.

As with all issues with children, if you think your teen is being bullied talk to them about it. They will be evasive but try and encourage them to talk, let them know you are there to help and listen when they are ready to talk. You can let them know you suspect what is happening and you can help to stop it. Explain the bully will never know how he was found out so things will definitely not get worse, only better. When your child eventually does tell all, however angry and upset you are, do not ring the parents of the bully or rush to confront him. Simply go and see the head teacher of the school the following day with all the information you have and ask what measures will be taken.

Your teen may well suffer from low self-esteem due to the bullying, so help to re-build his confidence and encourage some new friendships. Perhaps treat your teen and a couple of their friends to a night at the cinema and supper. Let your children know that you are always there to help and bullying is one of those things that will not necessarily go away on its own, so they must always ask for help. Explain that there is no shame or failure attached to being bullied, in fact it is quite the reverse – it is the bully who clearly has the problems.

truancy

Children who are bullied will often skip school; they would rather run the risk of being caught for playing truant than be taunted by the bullies. Other reasons for playing truant are boredom and falling behind academically, with perhaps learning difficulties such as dyslexia. Children who play truant will soon fall into petty crime, so if you know or suspect your teens are skipping school, tackle the problem immediately. Ring up the school and ask what their attendance has been over the past month, and if they confirm your worst fears, sit your child down and talk to get to the root of why they are avoiding school. If necessary, go and see the head teacher and discuss your child's problems. Perhaps they require special needs or extra coaching in a certain subject to catch up with the rest of the class.

honesty

Honest children can be confronted with whole new peer pressures when they become teenagers. Being supportive and open with your teenagers will give them not only the confidence to handle the new problems and pressures that will confront them but the confidence to talk to you about them.

By the time children have reached their teens they will have learnt what is right and wrong. They will know that lying and stealing are wrong but sadly, that is not to say that they will never indulge in either. Teenagers often don't necessarily tell their parents the whole truth but still think of themselves as honest.

'I've got a really bad stomach ache, Miss.'

Not unlike stealing, we don't want to have children who grow up lying to us or anyone else, so we have to encourage our children to tell the truth. The thought of our children growing up and becoming dishonest or deviant is one of a parent's worst nightmares.

Again, the best learning tool is a good example, but although we may think of ourselves as honest, upright citizens and good role models for our children, they just might perceive us differently. We constantly tell white lies so our teenagers can't see a problem in what they may perceive as a white lie, for instance, they may say they are going to their friend's house, when in fact they are going to a party.

When my daughter was sixteen, I was sorting out the washing when I found her student ID card. On close inspection I saw it said her birth date was 1984. 'Oh, they've made a mistake,' I thought, 'she was born in 1986.' When I pointed out to my daughter that this made her eighteen, she looked slightly embarrassed and then started laughing, 'It's meant to, it's a fake ID, mummy.'

With teenagers having so much more independence and freedom, there are whole chunks of their day when we probably don't know who they are with or where they are. As these are two of the most important and worrying factors with teens, it is important that we glean as much info out of them as possible. By remaining calm and trusting, we are more likely to be given this information, but if we are constantly judgemental and disapproving we will not.

stealing

The difference between young children taking somebody else's things and teenagers stealing is that teenagers understand very clearly about ownership.

No parent ever imagines that their beautiful bouncing baby will grow up to be dishonest. Have they bred a 'juvenile delinquent'? As frightening as the thought is, don't panic, even if your teenager has stolen something it does not mean they are earmarked for a life of hardened crime.

Here are some reasons why teenagers steal.

To Get What they Want

If teenagers have no allowance and you won't agree to buy something they desperately want they may go ahead and simply steal it.

PREVENTION

Make sure your teenagers have an allowance (see Money, page 76) and they know what is meant to be bought from it. If there is something they particularly suddenly want (and you will realize when that is), such as a new top for a special party or the latest CD by their favourite band, offer them some extra paid help around the house to help pay for it. By no means offer this as a solution every time, as none of us can have everything we think we need or want. And always make sure the task is completed (and done satisfactorily) before handing over the money.

Peer Pressure

Teenagers will often steal as a dare to prove themselves worthy of a certain peer group or just to show off and impress them.

PREVENTION

Teenagers who feel they are not worthy of their peer group may be suffering from low self-esteem and will need encouragement and praise to become more confident individuals. Explain that getting caught for shop-lifting and having a criminal record which may stop them being able to travel to certain countries during their gap year won't actually impress anyone.

Seeking Attention

Some children steal for attention and to be noticed. These children often lack self-esteem and perhaps have problems at school and receive little attention at home. Although the attention they will receive from their actions will not be the type of attention they would prefer, it will still be attention.

PREVENTION

As said above, teenagers with low self-esteem need encouragement and praise, but they must do something, however small or menial, to justify it. If they are stealing for attention they probably already know that it is wrong and it will be going against their parents' wishes, but it will certainly get the attention they crave, 'So finally, I'm getting noticed!'

Parents of teens lacking attention will have to examine the amount of attention or interest they pay to their teen.

Because they Can Get Away with it

Although parents should not overreact to children stealing, equally they should not underreact. Taking little or no action will hardly be putting out the message that they are never to steal again.

There was a recent case of a teenager who had been injured by the victim of a robbery he was committing and his mother, when interviewed, said, 'He didn't deserve to get hurt, he's not a bad lad, just a bit of a rogue.' Surely, we all want to cry out, 'Madam, wake up, your son is not a bit of a rogue, he is a dishonest, law-breaking thief who was trying to steal someone else's property!' But while parents adopt that type of attitude to their children's dishonesty, their behaviour is not going to change.

PREVENTION
Be consistent, take action if it happens and serve a punishment.

Fear of Dependency

Some teenagers fear being totally dependent on anyone ('The sooner the better,' you're probably thinking) so they take what they want to be self-sufficient.

PREVENTION
Ensure they have an allowance and perhaps take a Saturday or weekend job to feel more independent of the family.

Suspicions of Shoplifting

When teenagers are not at school their parents should know or at least have a very good idea, where they are, who they are with and what they are doing. Apply some common sense. If your teenager is out all day with little money and returns home with a new CD, question how they got it, don't put your head in the sand and shrug it off.

Likewise, if your teen keeps turning up with new items of clothing and some excuse about how they got them, ask to see the receipt. If they say they've lost it, insist next time they keep it and let you have it in case the item is faulty or washes badly and you can return it. Don't confront them and tell them you suspect them of stealing, because if they're not they will be very hurt and if they are they will deny it.

If you find new items of clothing in their room with a hole where the security tag has been cut out, explain that you were tidying their room and ask where they got the item of clothing and whether they have the receipt, because it has a hole in it and you'll take it back and get a replacement. You'll have a very good idea from their reaction what the truth is. If you have a good relationship with your teen, you could say in a very 'I know you'd never do anything wrong' voice that some people do shoplift and how appalling you think that is, explaining that people like that don't realize the seriousness of the offence and that they may as well go into the shop owner's house and steal their money. Finish with something along the lines of 'At least I know you're honest and trustworthy and would never do anything like that.' The fact you are suspicious but still trusting might often be enough to shame them into stopping.

What to Do if your Teenager Steals

Having spoken to your teenager as above, if items keep appearing in your home which you know your teenager has not been able to afford, sit down with your teen and explain your concerns. Tell them that you know they are honest, but ask if these items are being taken from shops without paying, and for what reason. Stay calm and ask them simply to tell you the truth, then you can work out what you will do and as long as it stops, you will draw a line under it and move on. And it will not be mentioned again. Reiterate that you know they are honest people so it's best to get to the deep-rooted reason why they took things.

Never shout or scream as this will signal to your child that you have lost control, and whatever you say will be less effective.

It is very important that teenagers do not benefit from the theft in any way. The item will have to be returned when possible and paid for, either out of their allowance or by doing work around the house to pay it off. As well as a spoken apology to the shopkeeper, parents should insist their child sends a written apology.

Parents must then sit down with their child, one-to-one, no nosy siblings listening in, and ask them why they did what they did and whether they realize how wrong it is and how lucky they are not to have been caught by the shopkeeper and confronted by the police. Parents should not walk up and down giving the, 'What shame they've brought to the family, how could they after all that's been done for them,' lecture, and avoid name calling. However, it is important that the parent talks to their teen in a 'concerned, let's discuss this' tone and not an 'I understand everything' tone.

Parents must explain that they can always come to them with any problems, no matter what it is; that there is nothing that cannot be discussed. Do not lecture and predict a life of crime or call your teen a thief or a bad person; it is the act they committed that was bad.

Parents should also consider if they have been too busy to give their teen any attention recently, or if there have been any changes in their lives that may have caused the problem. However, do not offer excuses as this will only negate your disapproval of their actions.

Once the incident has been dealt with, move on and **do not** discuss it again.

If teens persist in stealing then parents need to seek professional help.

Shoplifting and the Law for Under-Eighteens

For a first offence, if a teenager is caught stealing from a shop, the police will be called and the teenager will be taken to the manager's office to be questioned. They will be arrested and given a formal caution, unless the shop wants to press charges. A caution will go on record at the police station but the teenager will not have a criminal record. Parents or guardians will be called in.

However, if the store wishes to press charges, teenagers will be taken to a police station. The custody sergeant will decide if the teenager will be detained for further investigation. Parents will be called and a solicitor can be present whilst the teenager is read their rights and interviewed. They will also be fingerprinted, photographed and have their DNA taken. During the interview, if the accused admits to the offence or is a first offender, usually they will receive a formal caution and be released. If, however, it is the third or fourth offence they will be charged and a court date will be set. The punishment is usually a fine and community service.

lying

Not unlike stealing, we hate the thought of our teenagers lying to us or anyone else. The thought of our children being dishonest and deviant is another parental nightmare.

White Lies

White lies are part of everyday life. They are not said with the intention to cause malice or harm. They are just sometimes convenient, tactful and polite.

What husband with a modicum of self-preservation has never told a white lie to his wife's question, 'Does this dress make me look fat?'

Teenagers will certainly have grasped the concept of white lies but may stretch them to their outermost limits. If you suspect that a white lie has tipped over to a major lie, ask them outright, 'Now, is that absolutely, honestly the truth, on your honour?'

Here are some reasons why teenagers lie.

Privacy

Normally very honest teenagers may lie to protect their privacy. They may not feel ready for a barrage of questions if they have just started a relationship with a member of the opposite sex. This doesn't mean that they will never tell you, it just means that they are not ready to divulge certain information yet.

SOLUTION
If you start asking questions and they seem embarrassed or reticent to talk about it, leave it, don't pester them. Say something like, 'Well, if you want to talk about it, you know I'm here.'

Disapproval

Teenagers may also lie about where they are going or who they are going with if they think you will disapprove and stop them.

SOLUTION
Try to get to know their friends. Tell your teenagers to invite a few friends around for pizza and a video. If lines of communication have always been good between you and your children they are more likely to tell you where they are going, even if they suspect you will disapprove. Constantly judging their friends and calling them unsuitable and trying to dissuade your children from seeing them is only likely to strengthen their desire to do so.

To Avoid Punishment

If they know they are going to be shouted at, called names and given a harsh punishment as soon as they own up to a deed, they will deny it.

PREVENTION

As children, you hopefully taught them to always own up and that you would be far angrier with them (whatever they did) if they didn't tell you and you found out.

But as they get older, children must also learn to take responsibility for the consequences of their actions. For example, if your son owns up to breaking your favourite mirror by kicking a football around the sitting room, thank him for telling you but also tell him he should have known better than to play football in the house and he will have to put some of his allowance for the next month towards it.

Explain that 'honesty is the best policy' and however awful they think the consequences of an intentional or unintentional action may be, you would be very angry if you find out you have not been told the truth. Emphasize that there is nothing they could do that they can't tell you about. Your attitude to them as teenagers will gauge exactly how much they will admit. Parents who scream, rant and rave may well exacerbate the problem and as well as causing teenagers to deny their actions, they may well lie that someone else did it. This has serious repercussions for an innocent party and must be discouraged.

Teenagers need to understand how lies can devastate people's lives. Tell them that work, relationships and even people's freedom can all be affected by lies and give them an example. Even though it is unlikely that your child's lie is going to put anyone behind bars (hopefully), they should hear the consequences of where lying can lead.

To Hide Inadequacies

Parents should not have unrealistic expectations of their children as this can often be the cause of lying and even cheating during tests and exams. For instance, if a father expects his son to get an A grade in his maths exam and he only receives a C, he may well lie about the grade to avoid his father's displeasure and disappointment, even though the boy knows that his father will eventually find out. Lying simply delays the unpleasantness. Cheating may help him achieve the desired grade but is worthless if it was obtained through dishonesty.

PREVENTION
Make sure that you don't set such high standards that your children feel under enormous pressure to deliver and may resort to lying if they don't.

Peer Pressure

Teenagers are desperate to fit in with a crowd. They may tell untruthful stories to impress classmates, such as they smoke or have tried drugs or have already had sex, simply to be the centre of attention or because they suffer from low self-esteem and simply don't think anyone would be interested in them if they were just themselves.

PREVENTION
Help your teen to improve his self-esteem. If your teens are confident with their friends and realize that they are liked for who they are, they will be less likely to feel they have to impress anyone.

To Get What They Want

Teenagers will sometimes lie to get what they want but if challenged will often admit to their inaccuracies. They may say they have finished tidying their room, when actually they haven't, so they can go out with their friends, but this is a fairly mild lie, as a visit to the room will immediately prove otherwise.

In this type of incident, teenagers are more likely to think they are pushing their luck rather than telling outright lies.

PREVENTION

If you suspect or can prove that they may be stretching the truth, confront them about it and simply remind them not to lie to you. Impose some type of mild penalty more as a reminder than a punishment. For instance, with the above example, get them to finish tidying up their room and vacuum not only their own bedroom but yours as well.

Explain that if they had been honest to start with and asked if they could see their friends now and promise to finish their room later, you would have probably let them.

Lying for Attention

Teenagers who may be lacking in parental or social attention may conjure up elaborate stories and tales to attract attention. When they see this ploy works they will continue.

PREVENTION

Parents pretty quickly cotton on if their teens are telling elaborate stories for attention, so when you have proof, take them aside on a one-to-one basis and tell them that you know the story was an untruth. Avoid asking why they have been telling lies as it will probably prompt another one. After all, how many children are going to recognize their problem and say, 'Well, Mother, it's like this. I'm simply not getting enough of the right type of attention at home, and this seems to be a fairly successful way of attracting it.'

Self-fulfilling Prophecy

If a parent constantly tells their teenager, 'You're a liar,' then the teenager may well start to lie as they have already been labelled one. Teenagers may be vague about their whereabouts or change their arrangements at the last moment and decline to tell their parents, but when the parent finds out, the child is labelled a liar.

PREVENTION

Never call your teenager a liar, even if you suspect they have been, just let them know that you always need to know where they are or who they are with for safety reasons, and say that you know they are responsible enough to let you know in future.

'I don't think you've been entirely truthful,' 'There appears to be some discrepancy between what you should have told me and what you said,' are a good way to start, but never say, 'You're a liar,' or 'You lied to me,' if you want to encourage honesty.

What to Do if a Teenager Lies

If you suspect your daughter has lied take her aside and sit down with her. Standing up, towering over her can be far too intimidating. Ask her to tell you the truth about the particular situation, and explain that you will not be angry if she tells you exactly what happened. If she lied, she must own up and tell you, but if she doesn't and you find out she has lied, which you will, you will be angry. If your teens trust you to do as you say then in nearly all cases they will own up. If she is insistent that she did not lie, then you must accept it.

What parents perceive as lying, teenagers may perceive as white lies or being economical with the truth.

Explain to your teen how they could have avoided lying and that if they have a problem which they feel requires a lie, they should come and talk to you first.

Unfortunately, lying can become a habit very quickly, especially when teens realize that they can attract more attention and avoid taking responsibility for their actions.

> **Sam:** 'The only time I lied to my mum was about smoking, when I denied it. But when she found out, she didn't shout or get mad, she just said she was more upset about me lying to her than me smoking. It made me feel guilty when I denied it, and when she did find out, I felt stupid.'

Try and avoid falling into the trap of overlooking some lies, then punishing others. Be consistent. Explain that people who lie are eventually found out because of the inconsistency of their stories. It's easy to tell the truth and recall it but much harder to remember something that was invented.

Honesty at School

I can't imagine there is a person reading this who during their school years didn't tell a teacher at least one of the following:

- You'd left your homework at home when in fact it hadn't even been started.
- You weren't feeling well to get off games.
- You lied about the real reason that you were late.

Although it would be unrealistic to imagine we are ever going to stop teenagers wanting to try skiving off games on a freezing cold day, we can explain how honesty can minimize being reprimanded by teachers.

Take another example. If your son forgets to do his maths homework, suggest that rather than wait until the maths lesson starts to admit he doesn't have it (when the teacher can have a real go at him in front of the rest of the class) he could try to pre-empt the situation by going immediately to the staff room and being honest with the teacher … Your son should apologize and say when he will be handing in the work.

As soon as teenagers realize that honesty can diffuse issues, school life will run more smoothly.

eating disorders

The two eating disorders that terrify every parent are anorexia nervosa and bulimia nervosa. Both are psychiatric eating disorders which affect mainly young women but the condition is increasing among all young people. Both of these conditions usually start in adolescence and the outset of puberty, which are characterized by a preoccupation with food and a distortion of their body image. The biggest difference between anorexia and bulimia is that anorexics eat almost nothing while bulimics eat large amounts of food (binge eating) and then force themselves to vomit (purging).

Although girls tend to be more affected by anorexia and bulimia, some boys do suffer from these conditions, but because we think it is only girls, their condition sometimes goes undetected. Boys seem to want to appear more athletically shaped than just thin.

The third disorder is compulsive overeating.

What Causes a Teenager to Become Anorexic or Bulimic?

Parents and friends of anorexics and bulimics will try and find the defining moment or problem that led to this destructive condition but sadly, there probably isn't one, which it makes it even harder for parents to come to terms with it. Which leads them to think that without knowing the cause how do you find the solution?

Anorexia Nervosa

WHAT IS IT?

Anorexia nervosa is the relentless pursuit of a thin body and even when the sufferer is thin, they still see themselves as fat.

However, there are factors that have been identified in sufferers of this condition:

- They are usually perfectionists and high achievers at school.
- They suffer low self-esteem, although outwardly they appear to be confident.
- Their parents have high, unrealistic expectations, whether academic, sporting or social, which can cause teenagers to feel worthless when they cannot live up to them.
- They are constantly criticized by parents over their physical appearance.
- They need to feel in control over themselves and their lives. They have difficulty in expressing their feelings.
- They may be associated with activities where thinness is an advantage, like modelling, dancing or acting.

WARNING SIGNS TO LOOK OUT FOR
- Pushing food around the plate and eating very little.
- Fear of gaining weight.
- Losing weight and still insisting on dieting.
- Unhappy with their body shape.
- Knowing the calorific content of most foods.
- Unable to concentrate and a lack of energy.

- Depression, mood swings.
- Loss of periods.
- Excessive exercising, where it has become more obsessive than fun.
- Withdrawing from normal social activities.

Long-term effects of anorexia are very degenerative. The brain believes (rightly) the body is starving and slows everything down: the pulse, heart-rate and blood pressure. Brittle bones (osteoporosis), swollen joints and anaemia are also common. Severe cases can cause hair to drop out, fingernails to break off and tragically, as we all know, some cases lead to death.

Bulimia Nervosa

WHAT IS IT?
Bulimia is characterized by eating huge amounts of usually high-calorie 'comfort-type foods', known as bingeing, followed by inappropriate methods of getting rid of it, called purging, by either self-induced vomiting or using laxatives.

The bingeing is never related to actual hunger. Sufferers usually feel very guilty and depressed after a binge and purge to alleviate the feelings.

Some contributing factors which can make a person vulnerable to bulimia are:

- Pressure to be and remain a high achiever.
- Low self-esteem.
- Unhappiness about one's body shape.
- Depression, stress.

It is harder to determine if someone is bulimic as most of them are of normal weight, and some are even overweight. Bingeing and purging is also often done in secret making it much harder to detect a sufferer.

WARNING SIGNS TO LOOK OUT FOR
- Rushing to the toilet immediately after a meal.
- Spending long periods in the toilet, perhaps with the taps running.
- Bingeing on biscuits, cereals, ice-cream, etc, perhaps ten minutes after a proper meal.
- Evidence in the bin of empty cereal and cake boxes, biscuit wrappers, etc.
- Evidence of boxes of diuretics and laxatives in their room.
- Eats huge amounts of food but doesn't gain weight.

Long-term effects of bulimia are stomach ulcers, erosion of tooth enamel and tooth decay due to the gastric acids passing through the mouth with the constant vomiting, plus swollen cheeks and soreness in the salivary glands, irregular heartbeat, dehydration, loss of periods. Again, in very severe conditions the loss of the mineral potassium can eventually lead to heart problems and death.

Compulsive Overeating

WHAT IS IT?
Compulsive overeating is characterized by uncontrollable overeating or bingeing to the point of being uncomfortably full. During the bingeing sufferers may have a

pressured, frenzied feeling. Typically, the bingeing is followed by feelings of guilt, shame and depression which can lead to more bingeing. Unlike bulimics, sufferers of compulsive eating do not purge themselves after eating and therefore put on vast amounts of weight. Twice as many women as men are affected.

Some factors which make a person vulnerable to compulsive overeating are:

- Hiding away from their emotions.
- Low self-esteem.
- Constant need for love and approval.
- Feelings of worthlessness.
- Difficulty dealing with daily stress.

WARNING SIGNS TO LOOK OUT FOR
- Eating large amount of food when not hungry.
- Eating very fast.
- Eating alone.
- Depression and guilt after eating.
- Excessive weight gain.

If this condition is not dealt with it will lead to very serious long-term health problems including heart disease, depression, high cholesterol, kidney disease, arthritis and stroke.

How to Try and Prevent the Conditions

Although we know that some teenagers are more vulnerable to anorexia and bulimia than others, there are things as parents we can do to reduce the risk of this condition taking hold.

- Don't criticize your teenager's body shape.
- Be positive about their good points and help build their self-esteem about their physical appearance and academic ability.
- Don't give them unrealistic expectations that they will not be able to achieve and will leave them feeling worthless.
- Set a good example by not constantly talking about diets and trying different diets yourself.

Try and eat around a table as a family as often as possible, so that you can see exactly what your teenager is eating. You will also have better communication so you will be able to see if your teenager has suddenly become depressed or lethargic.

Hope

However, there is good news: eating disorders can be cured. Obviously, the quicker the problem is diagnosed the quicker and easier it will be to help the sufferer. Like all bad habits, the sooner the problem is tackled, the less time it will have had to take a real hold. The hardest part may be getting the sufferer to realize they have a problem, as anorexics and bulimics will be in denial. But if you are sure your child is suffering, seek immediate help.

The road to good eating and better health will not happen overnight and it will take a team effort of usually a nutritionist, a doctor and a therapist, and huge support from family and friends.

IF YOUR CHILDREN SUSPECT THAT ONE OF THEIR FRIENDS HAS AN EATING DISORDER WHAT CAN THEY DO TO HELP?

Teenagers spend more time with their friends at school and at weekends than their parents so they are in a far better position to notice any of the above symptoms.

If they mention to you that they are concerned but don't know what to do, offer the following advice:

- Suggest that they speak one-to-one to their friend, voicing their concerns but not in front of other people.
- Let them explain that they know how easily it can start but as a friend they want to help.
- They could offer to make the first phone call for counselling and accompany them.
- They should build up their friend's self-esteem and let them know they are liked for who they are and what they are.
- Advise them not to talk about the disorder all the time.
- They should let someone in authority know of the problem. This is not snitching; it is showing a responsibility and concern for your friend.

drugs

One of any parent's biggest worries, along with teenage pregnancy, is drug abuse, and no matter where you live or where your children go to school, drugs are readily available. Although we obviously don't want our children to ever touch them, taking the 'it is absolutely forbidden', totally black and white attitude may not be the best approach for your children and may act like a red rag to a bull: 'If it's totally forbidden let's try it.' Equally, some parents believe that by talking about drugs to their teenagers it will influence them to try some, as if they'd never heard of them! Sorry, this is being totally naïve, all teenagers have heard about drugs.

If you regularly eat together, the issue of drugs will be raised, either by yourselves or by your adolescents who may wish to hear your views on the subject. If you express a very strong, inflexible opinion about drug taking, the chances are that should your teenagers ever try them or have a bad experience, they will certainly never admit it or feel they can discuss their fear with you. Explain that the only winner with drugs is the dealer, and they will try and get any child, however young, hooked to help fill their pockets. Let your children understand that these dealers are complete scum (just in case they got any ideas about filling their pockets).

Teenagers are desperate to take control of their own lives so the more you forbid something, the more likely they are to try it. However wonderful or sensible you think your child is, never underestimate the attraction of experimentation and peer pressure. When the subject comes up, don't blag or try to be cool about drugs: teach the risks, effects and the consequences of drugs and explain how to stay safe.

Read the information below so you are informed about the different drugs; you will lose their respect on the subject if you are more ignorant than they are about it.

Explain that possession of drugs can lead to being charged and that has consequences for the rest of their lives. A criminal record would prevent them being allowed to enter most countries in the world including the two popular favourites with young people, Australia and New Zealand. It would also make it difficult, if not impossible, depending on the sentence, to work or live in the USA, plus it can also prevent them from getting particular jobs they may want.

Your children without doubt will ask if you tried any drugs when you were young. Be honest, if you smoked cannabis, tell them, explain how it made you feel, why you did it.

When my children asked me, I admitted that I dragged on a few joints at parties when I was about nineteen, but I preferred having a drink, because with the hash everyone used to get so laid back they'd just sit around. At least with a drink they'd get up and dance. They immediately tested me by asking if it was all right if they tried it, and were pleasantly shocked when I said if they were ever offered a joint, once they were eighteen, they could try it, as long as it was definitely cannabis and not some other drug. I have explained that where I don't find the occasional puff of a shared joint particularly dangerous (and I know there will be those that disagree with me), I would ask them never to try a pill or needle as they have absolutely no idea what they are getting into. I described the appalling and fatal effects just one Ecstasy or heroin hit can have.

A few months later my eldest daughter said she had tried a joint at a party and said she agreed with what I had said about its over-relaxing values. As I started to talk to her about it, she hooted with laughter and said she hadn't really tried it, she just wanted to see what my reaction would be. She wanted to know if I really would be as relaxed about it as I had originally said. I could immediately see that my relaxed attitude reduced her 'need' to dare to try it.

Drug addiction rarely happens as a result of teenage experimentation but because of a much larger problem. Teenagers who have good communication with their parents and are given support to tackle difficulties themselves, will be far more able to cope with what life throws at them than children who have been overly protected or given very little guidance and support.

THERE ARE MANY REASONS WHY TEENAGERS TAKE DRUGS:

- Attempting to increase self-esteem.
- Anxiety.
- To escape family or other emotional problems.
- Out of curiosity.
- To appear cool to their friends.
- To fit in with a crowd.

Whatever the reasons, keep an open mind and let them know that you are approachable if they wish to talk about peer pressure to try it, or that they already have.

HOW TO TELL IF YOUR TEENAGER
HAS A DRUG PROBLEM

Many of these symptoms and situations are normal with teenagers so be vigilant and sensible in your diagnosis.

- Lethargy
- Appetite changes
- Mood changes
- Irritability or aggressiveness
- Loss of interest in normal social activities
- Lack of personal hygiene
- Shortage of cash, perhaps even taking your money
- Changes in their sleep pattern

OBJECTS TO LOOK OUT FOR
- Discoloured spoons (from heating)
- Tin foil
- Small pieces of cling film
- Sugar lumps
- Cigarette papers and cigarette ends made of card
- Butane canisters
- Shredded cigarettes
- Different pipes
- Syringes or needles
- Small plastic bottle with a glass tube in it

WHAT TO DO IF YOU SUSPECT YOUR TEENAGER
HAS A DRUG PROBLEM

Before you storm into their room and search for the evidence, which will immediately have the ramifications of you being deemed untrustworthy and nosy, sit down with your teenager and calmly tell them that you are concerned by their change in behaviour and as you have always been honest with them, you would like them to be honest with you. Describe what behavioural changes/money missing you have noticed. Explain that you are not going to go berserk; you are simply concerned and would like to offer your support and help, because continuous use of drugs has passed the safety of the occasional puff on a joint at parties, and no one can succeed in giving up on their own.

Be understanding, reassuring and supportive.

Avoid asking 'Why?' as it will immediately put your child on the defensive and you want them to open up and talk, not clam up. Ask questions beginning with 'How?' 'Where?' 'What?' and 'When?' Whatever the answers, don't raise eyebrows, make snide comments or be judgemental, just listen and gently coax out as much information as possible. Don't try and find out who or what to blame, it won't help the situation. And don't assume you know why, as this will only upset your teenager and it'll probably be wrong.

Make the focus of the conversation what you are both going to do about it, not what it's doing to you or your health. The important thing is they know they have your unstinting support, but they also have to put the effort in.

If you don't feel you will be able to talk to them without getting angry or upset then perhaps get the other parent, or their favourite uncle or god-parent to speak to them.

If you are not sure what to say, ring a parent or drug helpline and ask their advice. Never talk to your child whilst you are angry. Naturally, as the parent you will feel panic, anger and confusion but you don't want to relay any of these feelings to your child, who is no doubt feeling a great deal worse. And just because you've found some cigarette papers and a small amount of hash carelessly left in their jeans for the wash, don't give up and think their life is over, and they are addicts beyond help. They could easily be just experimenting and getting the occasional high with their friends. If you have a close relationship with your children and see them at the dinner table most evenings, you'll be able to notice a change in their behaviour and stop it before it gets too serious. Even if your child is addicted, don't give up on them, there is plenty of help and support available.

Websites that will help are www.talktofrank.com and www.pada.org.uk (parents against drug abuse).

> **Sam:** 'A good way to get out of peer pressure is to say, "My school is doing drug tests and the teachers are suspicious of me." That way you still sound cool and most people wouldn't argue if you've got a good reason.'

Cannabis

Cannabis also known as ganja, grass, hash, hashish, hemp, marijuana, shit, skunk, weed, smoke, backy, Bob Hope, black, blast and weed, to name but a few!

Cannabis is the most widely used illegal drug in Britain. It is fairly cheap and easily available.

APPEARANCE

It comes in different forms. Hash is a blacky-brown lump made from the resin of the plant, and it can sometimes be a bit squidgy. Grass or weed is made from the dried leaves of the plant and looks like packed dried garden herbs. Cannabis oil is a dark sticky liquid which usually comes in a small bottle and is smeared onto a cigarette paper to smoke.

Cannabis is usually mixed with tobacco and smoked in a hand-made roll-up called a joint or a spliff. It can also be smoked in a pipe while some people make tea or even put it into cakes.

EFFECTS

The effect of cannabis can range from feeling happy, relaxed and chilled out to feeling sick and paranoid. It does affect co-ordination so users should not drive or operate machinery. Someone who has been smoking a lot will have bloodshot eyes and will be constantly eating, which is known as 'having the munchies'.

Users of cannabis are more likely to get hooked on the tobacco they smoke with cannabis than the actual drug itself. Only about ten per cent of users become dependent. If it's only been used for a short while there should be no problem stopping and there are no physical withdrawal symptoms.

CANNABIS AND THE LAW

Cannabis is a Class C drug. It is illegal to have, give away or deal in Class C drugs. If an under-eighteen year old is caught in possession of the drug, they will be arrested, have their drugs confiscated and be taken to the police station for a formal warning. Their parent or guardian will be asked to attend. What happens will have a lot to do with their age, whether it is their first offence or if they are dealing.

Ecstasy

Otherwise known as E, brownies, burgers, disco biscuits, hug drug, 'Rolexes', Dolphins and XTC.

Ecstasy became popular in the early nineties among the rave culture. Clubbers took them so they could dance all night.

APPEARANCE

Known to chemists as MDMA, pure Ecstasy is a white crystalline powder but is usually sold on the streets in tablet form, although powder is becoming more popular. It may not always be white as Es are sold in all kinds of colours and may even have pictures or logos on them.

As with most drugs Ecstasy is often produced with cheaper ingredients such as amphetamines, caffeine and substances that you would find under your kitchen sink.

EFFECTS

Tablets are usually swallowed, although some people smoke or snort the powder. The effect will kick in after about thirty minutes and last for three to six hours and the user will feel very alert and buzzy, and very loving towards the people around them.

On the down side users can feel anxious, experience panic attacks, first-time epileptic fits, confusion and paranoia.

The drug raises the body temperature and increases the heart-rate. As users are usually dancing in a packed disco all night their body temperature rises dangerously high and they can suffer dehydration and double heat-stroke. Drinking too much, even water, can be fatal as Ecstasy causes the body to release a hormone which arrests the production of urine, so drinking too much too quickly interferes with the body's salt balance and can be as fatal as not drinking enough. Since 1996 there have been over 200 deaths from Ecstasy.

Ecstasy is not addictive but continuous use will cause the user to build up an intolerance, and they will therefore have to take more to achieve the same effect, which makes them more likely to develop a psychological dependency.

ECSTASY AND THE LAW
Ecstasy is a Class A drug and it is illegal to be in possession, to give it away to friends or to deal. Possession carries a jail sentence of up to seven years and in the eyes of the law giving an Ecstasy tablet to your friends is supplying and carries a jail sentence of up to life imprisonment and a hefty fine.

Cocaine

Cocaine is also known as Charlie, C, white and coke.

Cocaine is a stimulant with powerful but short-lived effects. Unfortunately, cocaine has got itself a name as being a glamour drug, partly because it is commonly associated with music, TV and film stars, and partly because it is has an exaggerated reputation of being cut with credit cards and snorted through rolled up £50 notes. Having a high street value immediately qualifies it for being padded out with talcum powder, sugar and starch. And like most drugs some of the contents would be usually found in the kitchen cleaning cupboard.

APPEARANCE

Coke is a white powder that is usually cut into lines by a razor blade and snorted through a rolled up bank note or a straw. It can also be snorted off small spoons. Sometimes cocaine is smoked or diluted and injected.

EFFECTS

Cocaine makes users feel on top of the world, confident and aware. It raises the body temperature, increases the heartbeat and staves off feelings of hunger. But it only lasts approximately twenty to thirty minutes. The problem with coke is when the effects wear off there's an immediate temptation to have some more and this is what makes it so addictive. It's a difficult habit to kick as dependents feel so low and very rough after stopping they are soon tempted back.

Long-term use will cause depression, paranoia and anxiety. Sniffing too much coke will result in the nasal lining disintegrating and a lower sex drive. Death can occur from overdoses, and users who have heart problems or high blood pressure are putting themselves at a higher risk of heart attacks.

COCAINE AND THE LAW

Cocaine is a Class A drug and possession carries up to a seven-year jail sentence. Supplying, or even sharing it with your friends (the same in the eyes of the law) carries a maximum life sentence.

Crack Cocaine

Crack is a form of cocaine made from cocaine, baking soda (yes, baking soda) and water. It is called crack because of the cracking sound it makes when it's burnt. It is a powerful stimulant with short-lived effects and very, very addictive.

APPEARANCE

Small lumps or rocks about the size of a raisin. It is usually smoked in a pipe, glass tube, plastic bottle or in foil. These methods are known as freebasing. It can also be injected.

EFFECTS

The effects are the same as cocaine but much more powerful and shorter lived, just a couple of minutes peaking then in total about ten minutes. It is a much more powerful crash, with the user desperately craving more. Hallucinations, mood swings and serious paranoia can accompany the highs with some users becoming violent and aggressive. During the lows users become depressed, tired and feel ill.

Death from crack occurs through overdosing, mixing the drug with other drugs such as heroin and alcohol. It is highly addictive and very difficult to control.

CRACK AND THE LAW

Another Class A drug, illegal to possess, share or sell. Possession carries a seven year sentence and supplying can carry life imprisonment.

Heroin

Also known as 'brown' although many users incorrectly think 'brown' is non-addictive. It is an opiate made from morphine from the opium poppy and is a very strong painkiller. It is either smoked, snorted, or dissolved in water and injected. A heroin habit can cost up to £100 a day and very often users turn to crime to fund it.

APPEARANCE

Pure uncut heroin, the type doctors prescribe, is a white powder. But because of its high street value heroin available from dealers has been cut with anything from talcum powder to ground-up gravel and can appear any shade of white to brown.

EFFECTS

Heroin stops physical and psychological pain by slowing down the body processes. Users usually get an initial rush or buzz as soon as they take it and a small dose would leave the user with a feeling of well-being. Larger doses will make the user sleepy or very relaxed.

The chances of getting hooked on heroin are very high. Users have to take more and more to get the hit they crave and even more to feel 'normal'. Users suffer physical and psychological dependency. Drugs have been developed to help treat heroin addiction.

Deaths occur from overdose of the drug on its own, mixing with alcohol, taking other drugs with it and respiratory failure. Death can also occur from choking on vomit as the heroin stops the body's cough reflex working properly. Users who constantly use syringes run the risk of vein damage and even gangrene and HIV/AIDS by sharing dirty needles.

HEROIN AND THE LAW

Heroin is a Class A drug. Possession can lead to a seven year prison sentence. Supplying or giving it to a friend could lead to life imprisonment and an unlimited fine.

smoking

Regardless of all the health warnings about the dangers of smoking, teenagers continue to light up, and even the clear, large black letters stating **SMOKING KILLS** on each packet is not enough to deter them. Statistics that prove that one third of all people who smoke, die from it, makes little impact. Teenagers don't think that way, because at this age they believe they will live forever; the age of their parents and grandparents is beyond their comprehension. If you mention the problems associated with smoking, such as cancer or strokes, they think they'll find a cure by the time/if they get it, not that they will. If you mention to girls how inhaling smoke will dry up and line their skin, they say they can have botox and cosmetic surgery. They believe they are in control, they can handle it, they won't

become addicted. And 'the addiction' is perhaps the only way we can offer reasons not to start.

WHY DO TEENAGERS START SMOKING?

It's not rocket science why teenagers smoke, they think it's adult and cool and there is huge peer pressure for them to start. It's one of those activities like sex that is always associated with being adult. And smoking and sex is a very adult combination. How many movies do we see where the real heroes or villains smoke, how many film scenes have there been when the star exhales slowly and pleasingly on a cigar? And how many more films do they see where people light-up after 'great' sex. Which reminds me of the joke about the guy who asked a woman at a party, 'Do you smoke after sex?' to which she replied, 'I don't know, I've never looked.' Anyway, our teenager smoking is no laughing matter.

WHAT CAN WE DO ABOUT IT?

Telling your teenagers they shouldn't smoke is a fairly fruitless exercise, it's immediately imposing the 'I'm the parent, you're the child and I know best' attitude, which particularly gets their backs up and will immediately have them storming off or closing their ears or denying that they do smoke.

Point out to your teenagers that you realize lots of their friends smoke and what concerns you, apart from their health, is the fear of addiction – this is the part they will not understand, and why should they.

Explain face to face that smoking becomes non-optional. They won't just smoke, they will become smokers. Smoking will become their lifestyle. They will believe they can give up whenever they like, but they are very much mistaken. They may live their entire life believing they can give up cigarettes, and even if they manage it with the aid of patches or other treatments, not a day will go by when they won't think about smoking. Then there is the danger that the slightest amount of stress will be the trigger for them to start again. It's no different to alcoholics.

With more and more public places becoming non-smoking, the smoker has to plan when and where they will be able to smoke. The enjoyment of seeing a film at the cinema will be ruined by the thought of when they can get outside to have a cigarette. They'll end up one of those sad people who have to stand in freezing cold doorways because of no-smoking policies in offices. Restaurants, aeroplanes, shops, trains and no doubt eventually (hopefully) pubs are all non-smoking, so where are they going to smoke? It's no longer a social thing to do. In fact it is very anti-social and is the only addiction that directly affects someone else. A drug addict may shoot up next to you and it will not affect you, an alcoholic may drink next to you and it will not affect you, but a smoker will light up and not only will you become a passive smoker, your hair and clothes will smell of it.

Not only can smoking seriously affect their health but it can seriously affect their wealth, or lack of it.

If, of course, your children have grown up watching you smoke, then it is fairly natural that they will follow your example. Children are far more likely to do as you do rather than as you say, despite what you tell them. If you don't smoke, do not allow your teenagers to smoke in your home, even if you know they smoke when they are out.

You can try explaining that smoking is so addictive that they will even smoke when they are sick – during the Bosnian war people would trade food for cigarettes even though their families were starving.

THE ONLY WINNER

The only people who are totally happy with cigarette addiction are the tobacco companies. They spend millions of pounds learning and studying teenagers so that they can manipulate them into starting to smoke.

Try explaining to your teenager just how much they will spend on smoking, and tot up for them just how much more they would have to spend a year on clothes, CDs, DVDs, clubs, etc if they didn't smoke.

FINAL WORD ON SMOKING

At the end of the day the best way to try and get your teenagers not to smoke is mirrored in many other areas of their developing life. Give them the responsibility to make their own choice about their future. After explaining about the downside of addiction, tell them they are intelligent and responsible, they are what they choose to be, you respect them to choose wisely.

drinking

With increased reports of binge drinking among teenagers, alcohol is yet another problem we have to cope with in relation to our children, but a healthy understanding of alcohol and ways to enjoy it in moderation are better than heralding it the 'demon drink never to pass their lips'.

Like smoking and sex, drinking is seen as an adult activity and the more we try to stop our children from drinking, the more they will feel the need to try it behind our backs. So I am a great believer in showing your teenagers that you feel they are responsible enough to try it by introducing them into drinking at home. The more respect they have for something the less likely they are to abuse it.

Once your teenagers are about fourteen, if you are having a special celebration at home or are out to dinner, ask them if they would like a little wine mixed with water to drink. The French have always brought their children up this way and they seem to have avoided the culture of binge-drinking. What it does do is show your respect for your teenager in that you judge they are grown up enough to cope with it. Invariably, they won't even like the taste and will stick with water or juice. But if teenagers are offered alcohol by their parents, the need to go and try it behind their backs loses its appeal.

Once your teenagers are actually imbibing (very modestly) with you, it is very easy to bring up the best ways to cope with social drinking. In being offered alcohol by their parents in an adult environment, your children will feel that you are accepting them as adults and trust them to drink responsibly. If they are sixteen and ask for a drink and are automatically told, 'Of course not, you're only sixteen,' don't be surprised when they go and get wasted with a friend in the park.

If your children see you drinking in the home environment, perhaps even every day having a glass or two of wine with dinner, they are seeing an example of how wine is enjoyed. If they only ever see alcohol being drunk at parties or when they manage to get into bars they will see a completely different type of drinking and will follow that example.

Tell daughters who may be concerned about their weight how very fattening alcohol is and how bad it is for their skin.

Very few teenagers understand (and why should they) that the alcoholic content of a glass of wine is not the same as a glass of vodka. Because teenagers' taste buds are still developing and many will start on sweet wines, the drink manufacturers have cottoned on and now produce all types of alcopops, which are sweet drinks mixed with a spirit. Explain how the sweetness hides its alcoholic content.

When they start going out with their friends to pubs, explain how they can pace themselves by alternating each alcoholic drink with a glass of water. Tell the truth about some drinking myths:

- 'You won't get drunk if you don't mix your drinks.' Wrong. Drink enough alcohol and you will get drunk.
- 'If you drink good quality wine, you won't get drunk.' Wrong. And sadly I can vouch for this.
- 'Drink milk before you go out drinking and you won't get drunk.' Wrong. The milk will actually curdle with the acidic content of the alcohol.

Date Rape Drug

Sadly, we've all heard about date rape drugs being slipped into girls' drinks in bars and clubs which cause black-outs, loss of inhibition, disorientation and loss of consciousness.

Rohypnol, otherwise known as 'Roofies', and gamma hydroxylbutyric acid, known as GBH or liquid ecstasy, are both tasteless, odourless and colourless, so there is no way of knowing if it is in a drink.

Explain to your daughters how they can protect themselves.

- Never put down their drink, and keep it with them. If they put it down and it is out of sight for even just a few minutes, leave it and buy another one.
- Never accept an open drink from someone they don't know as trustworthy. Always watch the bartender pour or mix their drinks.
- Put their thumbs over the top of an open bottle if they are drinking from the bottle.
- Make a pact with their friends to all look out for each other and watch over each other's drinks if one goes for a dance or to the toilet.
- Don't take drinks from open punch bowls at parties unless it is a real friends-only gathering.
- If they suspect they or a friend has been given the drug, they should go immediately to a hospital emergency ward. They will experience tingling on the back of the neck and suddenly feel very drunk and disorientated. If they suspect who did it they should call the police.
- If they are not with friends, tell them to go into the ladies toilet, but do not lock the door, ring their parents or an adult friend, tell them their whereabouts and stay put until help arrives.

Why Teenagers Drink Heavily

Lack of parental support, lack of communication, inconsistent discipline and hostility towards teenagers are all causes of heavy drinking and alcohol-related problems in adolescents.

Peer pressure to drink certain drinks and/or too much is a constant problem. Many adolescents feel insecure about themselves and alcohol makes them feel more confident and less inhibited. A certain amount of alcohol can make them feel light-headed and fun. And enough alcohol makes worries and personal pain disappear (temporarily). Something adolescents don't seem to suffer with, that gets worse with age and teaches most of us to be very careful, is the good old hangover.

If your children suspect they have a friend who is drinking too much, tell them to talk to the friend to discuss their concern but if they are in denial to tell someone in authority at school or their parents (if they feel they will understand). Teenagers are very reticent about telling someone in authority as it looks like they are 'splitting' and will lose the friendship. But a real friend must get help. Explain that adults are not completely stupid and will not say how they found out. Families should easily be able to tell if one of their children is drinking heavily.

Drinking and Driving

Once your teens reach an age where they are going to bars to meet friends, make it absolutely clear to them that one thing they never, ever do is get into a car with a driver who has had an alcoholic drink. No matter what time of night it is or whatever the circumstances, they can ring you for a lift if the alternative is getting into the car with someone who has had a drink.

And once they start driving, explain that if they drive they simply don't drink, not even one. Break that rule and the use of the car goes for a month.

Minor Teenage Issues

sibling rivalry

Rivalry and jealousy between teenage siblings is normal and the only thing parents can do is make sure they say or do nothing to give reasons to inflame them. Be aware never to overpraise one whilst criticizing the other, such as, 'I don't know why you find biology so difficult, your sister is so good at it'.

Young teenage boys do fight and unless they are actually really hurting each other it's best to leave them alone, but they will have grown out of it by the time they are about fifteen. Siblings will often argue, but left to get on with it they will come to their own conclusion and stop – it's usually the noise which causes parents to intervene, or one running to a parent with accusations. Parents should avoid asking at all costs, 'Right, now both tell me what's going on in here,' as this will lead to raised voices and more pushing and shoving as each tries to get their story across. A more controlled approach would be, 'Come on guys, you're almost adults, sort this out between you.' However, if there is a need to find out what is going on, try this approach: 'I will ask you each to give your view of what is happening. When one is talking the other one must not interrupt, you will each have your time to speak. Is there any part of what I have just said that either of you don't understand?' Listen to each and ask them both how they think this problem can be overcome (it will be something of mind-blowing importance such as an argument over who is sitting where, which DVD to watch or one has accused the other of taking their CD). Listen to their decisions and when they both agree, leave. Always try and encourage teenagers to sort out their problems, otherwise parents just become judge and jury to their disagreements. And in a few years they won't have you to do their negotiating and compromising for them, so it's best they get in as much practice as possible.

chauffeuring

It's very hard to avoid being at the beck and call of your teenagers. They now have a certain independence and social life but are too young to drive and you might not live near a good public transport system. Teenagers do take their parents for granted, in fact, I sometimes think they believe we sit around just waiting for their next request. Very often they will ask to be given a lift somewhere. 'When?' 'Right now, please,' with no advance warning, although they've just spent an hour or two getting ready in their room. 'How are you getting home?' 'Please can you pick me up at midnight?' No thought that although you are only a 'saddo' parent you also might have a social life. We know teenagers are not very organized, so it's best to ask them to make sure they let you know well in advance if they need a lift, to where and at what time.

'Sure, I'll give you a lift, son.'

Don't become the parent taxi service for all your teen's friends. If you ferry them one week, another parent can do it the following week, otherwise you will also be taken for granted by all the friends. And if there is no other parent willing, then say that you will take them, but you expect them to come round at the weekend and clean the car. You will be surprised how happy they will be to oblige.

Even after arguments (if you have been drawn into one), whilst you're still feeling emotionally bruised, ten minutes later your teenager may ask for a lift as though the emotionally charged exchange had never happened. Don't always agree, although they will always expect you to. Explain calmly that you are so upset by the way you have just been spoken to that you simply don't want to. It is perfectly acceptable to let your teenager know in a calm voice that you are angry and upset with them. They will often immediately apologize, but it doesn't always make you feel better.

Giving constant lifts is part of being a parent but it doesn't have to be completely one-way (if you'll excuse the pun). Sure, you'll give them a lift to a party at the weekend, but only after they've done something for you, like emptying and re-filling the dishwasher, vacuuming the sitting room or doing some ironing. As parents, we have to prepare our children for the real world outside the home, and this is just another lesson: you do something for me and I'll do something for you. Although hopefully they will have also learnt the value put on an altruistic gesture.

> **Sam:** 'I think it's cool the way my mum and step-dad are willing to give me a lift most of the time I ask, and when my mum asks me to clean the office in exchange for a lift, I have no problems because then I don't feel I'm taking liberties. Just the fact that my mum knows I will help when she asks me, she doesn't ask me that often and I still get my lift.'

mobile phones

What did we do as teenagers without mobile phones? We used a public phone. But trying to get a teenager to understand that concept is like expecting us to imagine life without the wheel. They are inherently part of our culture and they certainly have their place in today's world, but like everything they have their advantages and disadvantages.

PROS

- Children can always ring to say where they are, why they are held up and what time they will be home.
- In an emergency they could call the police, fire brigade or ambulance.
- We can ring them to bring home a pint of milk, etc.
- Confiscation of phones is a positive punishment.

CONS

- Children are permanently on the phone to friends with little idea of the cost, some running up bills of hundreds of pounds.
- They run out of battery or have it turned off when you try to call them.
- Mobiles are easily lost, although most children would rather lose their granny than their phone.

Teenagers have no concept of how long they spend on the phone

Controlling Mobile Phone Bills

If your child is running up huge phone bills, take one or all of the following actions:

1. Put them onto pay-as-you-go. Explain what their allowance is each week and explain how many minutes of calling that works out to. Most teenagers, not unlike us, to be fair, have no idea how much a call or a text costs or the configuration of pricing.
2. Point out in words of one syllable that if they run out of money by Tuesday, there will be no more until the weekend. Stand your ground amid cries of 'Unfair!' 'You can't do that!' 'But I have to have it!' and 'What if there's an emergency?' Explain they will have to use public phone boxes or be allowed limited use on the

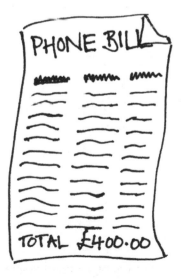

home phone. Even with no credit, they can still receive texts and calls, and can dial the emergency services. Give in once and you're training them that they can do it every time. Stand your ground and they'll learn very quickly. Explain that if you run out of money before the end of the month, you can't go to your boss and ask for some extra or for some of next month's salary now.

3. If they are not on pay-as-you-go there is a number which they can ring to see how many texts and minutes they have used. Let them know their monthly allowance and work out for them how many texts and minutes per day that equates to. Help them control it by checking with them each week. They'll soon suss it out.

4. If they constantly disregard their phone allowance despite explanations and warnings, simply take it away from them. No, they won't like it and yes, they will call you a few names. Ignore them, they don't mean them. You are the parent, you are paying the bills and your child is behaving irresponsibly and must learn there are consequences to pay. And this consequence is confiscation of the phone, their life-line (as they see it). Take it and hide it, if necessary at your work. The first time take it for a week. If the situation does not improve take it for two the next time. Remember, by taking this action you are helping your children to learn, not depriving them, regardless of what they say.

Showing Courtesy with a Mobile

We are all guilty of using our mobile in enclosed public places at one time or another, and if our children learn where and when they can happily use theirs, they need to be told. It's all about courtesy for other people. On public transport a phone ringing or someone speaking into one really annoys other travellers, so ask your children to turn off their ring tone. If they absolutely have to speak, tell them to whisper and keep the conversation to a minimum, as in, 'I'm on the train, I'll call later.' Or they could go into the area between carriages (which is hopefully quiet). They should also avoid using their mobile in restaurants, cinemas, theatres, even on busy pavements, in fact anywhere where people can overhear and might find it intrusive.

Explain that even playing games on their phones can create an invasive noise.

bedrooms

The bane of millions of parents' lives is the state of their teenager's bedrooms. Most parents have probably tried a combination of the following: threats, bribery, pleading, screaming, begging, and no doubt all with varying degrees of failure. Occasionally, when teenagers run out of clothes there might be a slight effort, or a few times a year there will be a total blitz, but on the day-to-day level, in most homes, teenagers' rooms are pretty abysmal.

Dirty knickers, clothes, screwed-up tissues all over the floor, drawers open with the entire contents spilling out, every surface covered in CDs, dirty plates and mugs, discarded snack packets and empty cans, and what is it with those wet towels? Let's face it, the only plus point is, if a burglar broke in he'd immediately think someone had beaten him to it and leave. But in the unlikely (hopefully) event of this happening, the state of our children's rooms does become our concern and although we could just shut the door and ignore it, we don't.

Now there are many areas and important issues which can cause friction between parents and adolescents so it's best to try and not add the bedroom fiasco to the list. However, while your teenagers are still living at home they should show respect, not only for your wishes, but also for their possessions.

Sadly, there is no magic formula that will suddenly transform untidy teenagers into 'tidy Marys' or 'Mrs Mopp' but there are some things we can do to make it as simple as possible for them to keep their rooms in an acceptable state. There is no point being over ambitious, so first, lower your standards considerably and prepare to be underwhelmed, because the only ones who become fraught and stressed over untidy bedrooms are us.

As soon as your child turns thirteen, suggest a makeover for their bedroom to provide a space that they can bring their friends. They may well want to get shot of the Winnie the Pooh duvet cover and matching curtains and get something more grown up. Plan a day out to go and choose a new colour scheme and bed linen, perhaps treat them to a few cushions and a lamp so hopefully they may start to take some pride in their room.

Don't worry too much about the walls, as you will slowly notice in daughters' rooms the pictures of fluffy kittens, ponies and dolphins disappearing to be replaced by posters of their teenage idols. And your teenage boys will no doubt soon be plastering their walls with posters of semi-naked girls. Some people view this as disrespectful to women, but I disagree, boys will learn how to respect women by the example shown by their parents, not by looking at a photo of a girl posing with a great figure, out of her own choice.

Explain that you will help them sort out old clothes and toys to make more space. Provide plenty of multi-functional hangers (the thick plastic types with double hooks) and show them exactly how to use them (you think I jest?). It's much easier to hang up jumpers and T-shirts than to try and fold them. If you can see the thought of hanging up clothes as too ambitious, treat them to two large but different laundry baskets or even new small colourful plastic dustbins and remove the lids. Explain which is the basket for dirty clothes and that only clothes in this bin/basket will be washed. The other bin/basket is for them to drop their clothes in on a daily basis instead of the floor, so this could for instance include the ten outfits they try on before going out and then discard, but are not in need of a wash. Obviously, the clothes will be creased next time they wish to wear them, but they would be if they were on the floor, and at least in the bin they will not be walked over and you will have the pleasure of actually seeing the carpet you no doubt lovingly chose. Once a week help them to put away in cupboards the clothes that are in the bin. Explain, without lecturing, that now they are interested in clothes they should start to look after them, as they will look better and last longer.

Provide large waste bins and ask that tissues, snack packets, cans, etc be thrown away. Give daughters a plastic make-up organizer so they can keep all their make-up together. Help them to keep CDs tidy by letting them choose a stand or case for them. Buy them some plastic draw dividers for their underwear, tights and socks.

From the age of fifteen, show your teenagers how to use the washing machine. Explain how to divide washes into colours and whites and how to dry different garments. Demonstrate how to iron different items at different temperatures and most importantly show them how to avoid losing their fingers when they fold down the ironing board.

Most importantly, if they don't already have one, treat them to a large mirror you can attach to the wall, so they can check out what they look like, sing in front of it, practise talking to people they fancy, check out how they dance, try different hairstyles and rehearse pop or film award acceptance speeches. If they don't have a mirror in

'It's normal – I'm a teenager!'

the bedroom they will spend longer in front of the bathroom mirror, no doubt at times when other members of
the family would like to be using it.

The one redeeming factor is that when they finally
move out and into their own home, they probably will be
tidy. After all, how many of us can honestly say we kept our
rooms tidy as teenagers? Do we now live in complete tips
now? I don't think so.

Katherine: 'Obviously I leave my room in a state; I'm
eighteen, it's expected. I'm proud to claim that I
couldn't date the average duration of a mug's life in
my room, though I think there is a clue to be found in
that many resemble the later stages of an Alexander
Fleming experiment. But, occasionally if asked, usually more than once, I can be brought upon to tidy it
eventually. And, regardless of what many parents
believe, I don't think a slightly untidy room results In
a downward spiral to heroin addiction and a life des-
tined for Holloway Prison, it's just clothes on the
floor.'

clothes

Firstly, before you start getting annoyed and disapproving
about what your teenager wants to wear or is wearing, look
out some old photos of yourself and your partner as
teenagers and stick them up in the kitchen, so that every
time you are about to have a go at them you can get a

'Oh my God, Mum. You're not going out dressed like that,
are you?'

reality check and remember what you looked like and how
much it disappointed your parents. No doubt you got over
it and so will they; this is their only chance to wear what
they like before they join the circus of the real world. Your
son may soon be saddled with a mortgage and a young
family and in a job which requires wearing a suit for the
rest of his working life, so does it really matter if he wears
those jeans with lime green shoes and his hair like that for
a few years while he can?

We have all been guilty at some stage of wearing clothes
that we probably shouldn't have and when teenagers start
to choose their own clothes, they may not be exactly what

we would choose for them. Whether they are wearing something to be fashionable, make a statement or be individual, think positively before you pass comment.

Try to avoid criticizing, so rather than the derogatory, 'What on earth are you wearing, those jeans look awful?' say something positive, such as, 'I preferred those trousers you were wearing the other day, you looked great in them.'

Teenagers are full of insecurities and anxieties, especially about their body shape and looks, so help to build their confidence. Everyone has good points so, for instance, when they bemoan the fact that they've got a fat waist, tell them not to worry because they've got drop-dead gorgeous legs.

If girls are wearing clothes that you feel make them look too old or too 'available', again forget the 'If you think you're going out looking like a tart, you've got another think coming,' approach and suggest a different top or a slightly longer skirt. Again it depends on where they are going. If they are going to a private party and are going to be dropped off and picked up by parents, then there is less risk than if they are travelling by public transport. If your daughter has just got to wear that particular skirt then suggest she wears a long coat for travelling to and fro or puts some track suit bottoms on for travelling and changes into the skirt when she arrives.

Show respect for your children by asking them what they think of something you're thinking of going out in. We all need a few words of reassurance sometimes and I often ask my children what they think of a particular outfit. They are always honest, and although it may not be the answer I was hoping for, it is the answer I was probably expecting.

Boys can be just as fastidious about their clothes as girls, so be equally encouraging and complimentary to them if you think they look good, 'Wow, you look fantastic, you'll have to ask those girls to form an orderly queue.' But be honest, and if you think the shirt doesn't really go with the sweater, in a very diplomatic way, suggest an alternative sweater.

It may come as a great compliment when your daughter begins to want to borrow your clothes, but first lay down a couple of rules. Always ask before they take anything and always have the courtesy to give it back on a hanger. Announce that if you find it on the floor you will be very angry, but try and avoid saying that if it happens she will never be allowed to wear anything of yours again, because quite frankly it's unrealistic. Explain that if she borrows a blouse it will need a wash afterwards so would they put it into the laundry basket. If it's a sweater, ask her to fold it and put it on your bed. If these rules are adhered to, the borrowing of each other's clothes will not be a problem.

Sisters Borrowing from Each Other

This can be a fairly explosive area and can cause any amount of rows.

Point out to your girls as soon as they start borrowing each other's things that they must ask each other and return or be responsible for getting the item washed and returned. You may well find that one sister will ask, while the other one just takes her sibling's things without asking and will leave them screwed up on her bedroom floor. It is better that you sit and talk this over with the errant sibling and try and get her to empathize. Regardless of whether they do or not, this type of behaviour is a no-no and if it happens again her allowance will be docked.

sleeping

'Just Another Five Minutes'

We all know that our teenagers like to stay up all night and sleep all day, and it drives us mad that when they've been up half the night watching TV or on their computer and they can't get out of bed in the morning for school. Having to go and wake them up repeatedly and tell them they'll be late for school is a stressful way for parents to have to start the day. It immediately causes animosity towards teenagers when a parent knows they did not go to bed at a reasonable time or when asked.

Teenagers need at least nine hours sleep a night for two very important reasons. First, during sleep a hormone is released which is essential for their growth and secondly, they will not be able to function correctly if they are sleep deprived.

Teenagers actually need more sleep than both children or adults but get less sleep than either.

Rather than moan about how lazy they are, there is now scientific evidence that suggests why they have nocturnal habits. Now, I know you're thinking, 'Pah! You don't need to be a bloody scientist to know that if you go to bed too late you can't get up in the morning!' And I am certainly not going to suggest that you inform them of the following information (oh no), but you just might have a better understanding of why they maintain the sleep patterns they have.

Adults produce increased levels of a hormone called melatonin at night and it is this hormone that makes us drowsy and able to sleep. Melatonin in adults kicks in at about 10pm, however, in teenagers, sleep laboratory tests discovered that this hormone does not start production until 1am. There are two reasons which may cause this:

1. Due to teenagers' habits of watching TV and playing on computers at night, they may be stimulating their brain to such a degree that melatonin production is delayed.
2. The development of hormones and the effects of puberty might actually cause the delayed production of melatonin.

Whichever it is, many teenagers suffer from sleep deprivation which can cause irritability, mood swings, inability to concentrate, aggression, antisocial behaviour, depression and lower academic performance.

At weekends and during school holidays let your teenagers lie in. Obviously, you don't want them to sleep all day as this will upset their body clock, so if they are not up at about midday get them up.

'To Sleep Perchance to Dream ...'

Rather like with toddlers, the best way to help your teenager get a good night's sleep is to help them establish a regular bedtime routine ('Is this woman mad?' you're probably thinking). The best way to do this is to talk to them and agree on a few ground rules. Make sure there are no younger siblings around when you are discussing bed times as they will want the same times. If necessary take your teenager out for supper to discuss it away from younger brothers and sisters.

- Sit down with your teenager and agree on a bed time. This will take some negotiation. Make sure you begin with an early bed time so you have room to compromise.
- Try to get your teen to agree to try and get their homework done early in the evening, as that way they can enjoy themselves and really relax during what's left of it.
- Explain that the agreed time for bedtime is the time they are in bed with lights, TV and phone off, not the time they start getting ready for bed.
- Make sure they don't drink caffeine-laced drinks or fizzy drinks during the evening, which will make it hard for them to sleep.
- For daughters, suggest a warm bath with some lavender oil and aromatherapy candles to wind down and relax before bedtime.
- Insist they stop using the computer half an hour before bedtime as, like caffeine, it over stimulates the brain, and suggest instead they listen to music, read or watch TV with you.
- Insist they turn their mobile phones off when they get into bed so they don't get disturbed by friends calling or texting.
- It's worth investing in a good feather pillow and duvet (for them and you) to make getting into bed a good experience. It really does make a difference.

Fran: 'Penny and I had a disagreement over what time I should be in bed on a school night. I suggested midnight, and she suggested 10pm (which I still maintain is ridiculous for a sixteen year old). After careful negotiation we decided that on two nights a week it would be 11pm, another two nights 10.30, and one night 10.45. (This plan fitted in nicely with what I wanted to watch on TV certain days a week). We also agreed that if I was too tired in the morning and couldn't get up we would make some nights earlier. To be honest, I don't always make it to bed at 10.30, but there isn't really much confrontation.'

Waking Them Up

There are ways to wake your teenager up which will start both your days in good temper, and ways which will get you both off to a grumpy, argumentative and resentful start. Knowing their bed time will be brought forward if they do not get up on time is certainly the incentive they need in our home, although first thing in the morning would not be the time to mention it; it has that ring of 'I told you so' about it which no one wants to hear first thing in the morning, if ever.

First, buy a loud alarm clock or radio alarm and set it for 20 minutes before they have to get up – most teenagers won't actually get up but they will have stirred.

THE LESS STRESSFUL WAY

- Stroke their cheek, speak their name and when they stir and half open their eyes, tell them that it is time to get up. Ask if they have heard what you have said and tell them you are going to put the light on or open the curtains.
- Say to them, 'You will get up, won't you, I don't want to have to come in again.' Wait for a reply or repeat the question until you get a reply.
- In five minutes, if you suspect they haven't got out of bed, knock on the door and ask if they are up. This will usually prompt them to get up.
- Still not up, then knock on the door, go in and wake them up again and get them to sit up with their legs over the side of the bed.

THE REALLY STRESSFUL WAY

- Shouting, 'How many times do I have to tell you to get up, I'm fed up with it every morning.'
- Threatening, 'If you don't get up in the next five minutes, you're not going out this weekend.'
- Name calling, 'Get your fat, lazy bum out of bed now!'

make-up

Most girls love to wear make-up – they've watched their mother applying it since they were born and simply can't wait to try it for themselves. No doubt you've already experienced them as very little girls getting hold of your lipstick and smearing it all over their faces.

Well, make-up, just like many other facets of teenage life, is something teenagers think they know all about and certainly do not want any interference from someone who actually does know what they are talking about. And to be fair, being a teenager is all about trying things out for yourself. However, as a parent, there are times when you simply have to intervene.

If your daughter is wearing so much make-up that it looks like it has been applied with a trowel and a spray can, it is your responsibility to say something. However, there are ways to avoid a head to head, so steer well clear of snapping something like, 'You're not going out with all that crap on your face,' as this will be lighting the blue touch paper. It will be taken as, 'You have no idea how to apply make-up,' and, as we all know, teenagers have ideas about everything. A sympathetic, more diplomatic way is to calmly suggest that they really don't need quite that much make-up as with their good looks a more natural style would be more attractive. Even offer to treat your daughter to a professional 'make-over' by a beautician at a local department store or beauty salon so she can see what suits her – if she agrees to go, tell her you are willing to treat her to a mascara and concealer (for instance). Prime the salon first that you want a natural look and ask them to compliment her good features. For instance, your daughter has beautiful green eyes but all she can see is her thin lips, so a compliment from an outsider may just be the confidence boost she needs.

Teenage girls do not need foundation all over their faces, but they probably do need a spot concealer. Dark, smoky eyes and deep red lips can be worn when they're older, but what they need now is lip gloss, mascara and maybe a soft coloured eye shadow for nights out. Lip liners, eyebrow liners and eyeliners are unnecessary for teenagers, but let the professionals tell them, as your advice will fall on deaf ears.

tattoos and body piercing

Tattooing has suddenly become quite fashionable (no, I can't understand it either). Celebrities and sports stars are now adorning their bodies with them so it is only natural that our impressionable teenagers will want to copy.

What your teenagers won't understand is that what may seem like a great idea now will not be such a great idea in five or ten year's time and the removal process is long and painful.

First, tattoo parlours must have permission from a parent if a child is under eighteen years old. If they are too young simply say no, but offer to discuss it again when they are sixteen or suggest they have a small henna tattoo to see if they like it. If they try it and are still keen when they are sixteen and you are still opposed, come to a compromise and see if they will agree to a very small, discreet one at the top of their thigh or below their knicker line.

Teenagers under the age of sixteen will need parental consent for any body piercing. Again, it's your taste against theirs, but if they insist they want body piercing, they must wait until they are fifteen and then you will compromise by saying that they will not be able to wear facial piercings to school, so they can have their tongue or belly-button pierced. Parental permission means parents accompanying their teenagers.

Fran: 'The main reason I would get a piercing is to see what my parent's reaction would be. I asked my parents if I could get my tongue pierced – expecting them to say no (and for me to get it done anyway). When their reply was 'Yes, but you have to pay for it,' the idea of having my tongue clamped and a metal bar being shoved through it kind of lost its appeal.'

homework

Another bane of every parent and child's school life. Although the ideal would be for them to get on with it as soon as they get back from school, now they are older this is harder to enforce, so to try and minimize the stress of having to continually ask (and then nag) them to do it by coming to a compromise at the beginning of each term. You ask them to work out exactly what time they will do it. If they appoint the hour, they are far more likely to stick to it. For instance, as soon as they get back from school, teenagers are usually starving, so they will want to crash out in front of the TV with a snack and a drink.

If they offer a homework club at school, try and get your teenagers to join, explaining to them the benefit of finishing all work at school, so they can come home and relax. A classroom is so much more conducive to work than a sofa in front of the TV. There is also no chance of them being unable to do it because they left something behind.

At home, whatever their age, they may need a little help organizing their work, so be helpful and encouraging. If they need help with answers, show them how to get to the answer without actually giving it to them.

If they are difficult to motivate and need organizing, help them to get organized and then stay in the same room whilst they're doing it.

If your teenager flatly refuses to do any homework, rather than work yourself up to a nervous breakdown, say, 'Fine it's up to you, I'll let your teacher deal with it.'

Fran: 'Parents must understand that sometimes teenagers just aren't in the mood to do homework. It doesn't mean your children are necessarily failing in school, they might just have had a bad day. Constant moaning does not act as an incentive to get the work done; it will just bring on stubbornness and arguments.'

swearing

As children get older, their vocabulary will become more rich and varied than you would probably prefer. TV, videos and films are the biggest source, followed by their peers and parents. Unfortunately, most of us use expletives fairly regularly at home without even noticing it.

Swearing is all part of the rites of passage of being a teenager; however, if they start swearing at home on a regular basis, do something about it. Tell them in a matter-of-fact way that if they are old enough to watch these movies which flaunt bad language, then they should be old enough to know not to use it at home. If they continue, don't rise to the bait and get angry, just immediately impose a punishment such as refusing them any TV or computer time for that day.

If your children have friends who use bad language in your home, simply inform them in a firm, 'no nonsense' voice that you do not allow language like that in your house. Teenagers will often swear more in front of their friends simply to show-off, so if you overhear it, simply ask them to stop, don't be sarcastic or try and humiliate them as this will make it far harder for them to back down.

But if your teenagers suddenly start using foul language on a very regular basis, regardless of what you say, there may be a deeper problem. Talk to them sympathetically to find out why they are so angry and discuss how their problem can be best dealt with or resolved.

Explain to your teens how offensive it is for other people to overhear bad language, so when they are anywhere in public, like streets, shops, buses, trains and cinemas, they should refrain from using it. If their friends start mouthing off they should just ask them to stop and if they are asked why, they could just mention that they can see their friends are pissing people off (said very quietly).

tvs and computers

As we all know teenagers will spend entire weeks in front of a TV or computer screen if possible. The way to cut down their time in front of a screen is to remove TVs from their bedrooms until they are about fifteen, otherwise young teenagers will watch it until they fall asleep. First, you will have no idea what they are watching and secondly, as TV is so visual, their brains will be too stimulated to let them fall asleep at their correct time and they will suffer from lack of sleep.

Insist that when you eat together, hopefully three or four times a week, there is a strict no TV rule, and also whilst they do their homework. That will immediately reduce their viewing by about two hours. Ignore their screams of, 'It's not fair!' If they are worried about missing their favourite soap while you eat, ask them to record it.

If you are worried about the time they are spending on their computer, come to an arrangement with them on how long is reasonable.

Safety and the Internet

And just when you thought they would be safe indoors, along comes the Internet, bringing the dangers of the chat room into your very home.

So although you can block sex and violence, chat rooms are a big attraction when it comes to that frisson of danger. For teenagers, contacting new 'friends' through the Internet is an exciting and new way of extending their social lives, and it can be done from home. The danger behind chat rooms is they have no idea if the person they are talking to is who they say they are. Paedophiles and sex abusers access chat rooms and pose as children to try and strike up friendships, with the sole intention of trying to persuade them to meet up.

Explain to your teens that they must come up with an imaginary nickname when they log on and, most importantly, however friendly they become with someone, **never to divulge their name, home or school address, mobile or home phone number, e-mail address and even the area where they live. Most importantly, they must never agree to meet up with someone they have met over the Internet.**

Find out whether your teenager's school has a school-only 'closed' chat room, that can only be accessed by pupils or friends of the pupils who have been given the web address.

Let your teenager know that if anyone is probing for personal info or asks to meet up to let you know. Speak calmly and be reasonable, as overreacting will prevent your children ever telling you anything. Also ask them not to open e-mails or files from names they don't recognize in case they are carrying viruses or porn material. Explain that you don't mind them using chat rooms but they must stay in the 'public area' and steer clear of 'whispering' – a way of sending a private message to an individual. Ask your children to always close down programmes when they have finished, as chat rooms and music channels used for down-loading are especially vulnerable to viruses which can corrupt your files.

This is exactly what happened when my stepdaughter, Francesca, left a music programme open all night on my computer. In the morning every file had been deleted, every word, everything. I know I should 'back-up' my files every evening, but I hadn't, and it took a computer whiz and £2000 to recover the material from the hard drive.

'Francesca … can I have a word …'

To prevent them accessing nudity, sex, violence and swearing follow the instructions supplied by your Internet service provider for parental controls. Alternatively, the following should work on any PC: click Start> Settings>Control panel>Internet options>Content>Enable ratings>Adjust ratings levels>provide password for security.

Glossary

Just so that you know what your teenager means when he uses certain words, here is a compilation put together by mine.

> **Fran:** 'Under no circumstances ever use any of these words. Parents who do are really embarrassing and lose all our respect.'

Whatever! – You're right but I don't want to agree with you
Rinse – Make fun out of someone
Cash-back – When something unexpectedly good happens
Safe – OK, good
Wot? – Pardon?
Urgh? – Wot?
Played – Well done
Gay – Stupid
Sound – Fine, that'll do nicely
Legend – A really, good, amazing funny, good-looking person, respected by many people

Player – A good guy who gets lots of girls
Ginga – redhead
Minger – not very attractive

Final Word

As children become teenagers they enter the last development stage of their lives that we are directly involved in, so this is our last chance to make a difference.

Our teenagers are on the launch pad of their adult lives, and these are the last few years before they leave home to follow their dreams and aspirations, taking our dreams for them away.

Have we done a good job? Have we made them the very best people we could?

We've so far given them everything we could from pedal cars to DVDs, but are they fully equipped for all those important occasions which will arise when they are finally unleashed into the adult world? Will they have every life skill to feel confident in any situation?

We, as parents, know what a tough world is waiting for them, and we want to give our children every opportunity to be able to flourish within it. Our responsibility is to impart the skills to our children which will help them live a confident and successful life.